Opposites ATTRACT

Understanding God's Design
for Lasting Relationships

To God be the Glory!

Karen Hampsch

Opposites ATTRACT

Understanding God's Design for Lasting Relationships

CARL HAMPSCH

DESTINY IMAGE® PUBLISHERS, INC.

P.O. Box 310, Shippensburg, PA 17257-0310

*"Speaking to the Purposes of God for this
Generation and for the Generations to Come."*

This book and all other Destiny Image, Revival Press, Mercy Place, Fresh Bread, Destiny Image Fiction, and Treasure House books are available at Christian bookstores and distributors worldwide.

For a U.S. bookstore nearest you, call 1-800-722-6774.

For more information on foreign distributors, call 717-532-3040.

Or reach us on the Internet: www.destinyimage.com

ISBN 10: 0-7684-2504-2
ISBN 13: 978-0-7684-2504-8

For Worldwide Distribution, Printed in the U.S.A.

1 2 3 4 5 6 7 8 9 10 11 / 09 08 07

Dedication

To my wonderful wife, Karen, God's perfect choice and balance for my life. We did it!

Acknowledgements

Ever hear the joke about the doctor "practicing" medicine? So much of what we learn about life and ministry is through the process of trial and error. Most of what Karen and I have come to understand has come through this sometimes painful but always impacting process.

I often think back to my early years of ministry when all I knew was theory, and the poor souls who endured my maturation. I am so grateful to the Body of Christ who has patiently listened and supported me while I tried to gather wisdom. I shutter when I think back at some of the sermons I had preached with great conviction, but with little experience. I prayerfully hope that the couples I counseled early on somehow survived my zeal and were sustained by the Lord. Praise God for all the precious sheep who have faithfully followed as I have tried to learn the shepherding skills needed to lead the flock and teach them God's ways.

God's love is an amazing thing! The Bible tells us that it "knits us together." What a beautiful picture of lives intertwined with a strength and warmth that comes from that unity.

I am so blessed to have been surrounded by such wonderful and supportive friends and loved ones who have let me "practice" on them.

Most of all I am eternally thankful for God's grace, His underserved favor! His grace has covered our lives and sheltered us in the darkest of storms, and the times when hope's light in our ministry and our marriage seemed to be fading. His grace truly is sufficient for us!

Endorsements

It really is true that opposites attract. In this straightforward but humorous book, Carl Hampsch does a masterful job of helping married couples understand and beneficially utilize their God-given differences. You may be surprised to discover that your husband or wife is not the only marriage partner in the world who is continually testing his or her spouse's patience, seemingly pushing them beyond their comfort zone, or constantly holding the other back from the things he or she is really called to. In this book, Carl identifies many of the conflicts and disappointments that couples face due to differences, and perhaps more importantly, he will help you learn God's ways of dealing with those differences.

Opposites Attract will show you how to turn an unpleasant and disappointing situation into a truly blessed and fulfilled marriage. I highly recommend this book for every married couple.

Craig Hill
Founder of Family Foundations International
and author of *The Ancient Paths*

I laughed, I cried, I even rolled my eyes! I could really relate to his stories. They sound so familiar!

Karen Hampsch
(author's wife)

Table of Contents

Foreword

In the classic film, *Mary Poppins*, Julie Andrews sings, "Just a spoonful of sugar makes the medicine go down," and we love it. Similarly, Carl "sings" in this book, "A little bit of humor makes the hard words go down"—and you'll love it.

I have been a marriage (and other things) counselor for more than 40 years. I know everything Carl writes here, backward and forward. So when Carl first asked me to read his manuscript, I told myself, "Carl's a friend. Grit your teeth and hang with the reading even though it's old hat to you"—but I couldn't put the book down! Carl spices wisdom with such delightful ways of saying things and such self-deprecating humor that you can't help identifying with him and Karen to find yourself seeing your own crossover battlegrounds, and laughing at them—and at yourself.

At Elijah House we have often taught that God seldom brings together couples who can get along; He always brings together opposites perfectly designed to grind on each other! Then we show how bitter root judgments and expectancies draw us to each other and exacerbate all our problems, until we either give up and quit the marriage or we die to self, and He turns our differences to blessings. We have hoped that our students—or counselees, as the case may be—can hang in there long enough to take home tough truths for transformation so as to be changed by the merciful ministry of our Lord Jesus. Sometimes, to our chagrin, people bail out, unwilling to face all those tough truths and pay the price of eating humble pie and dying on the cross to allow God to change them.

The delightful thing about Carl's book is that he makes those painful insights fun to see, and healing results. His insights are so right-on that it's difficult to dodge the bullets of truth that bring us to death on the cross. Yet what is different about Carl's writing is that you'll find yourself enjoying the process; whereas heretofore it may have been almost too painful to continue.

Many writers lay out valuable truths for living—and dying. But to me all too many postulate grand theories that may or may not be relevant—if only you could decipher what those grand words mean! Carl states deep theories, yet goes past theory into reality in such "down home" language that even a spiritual klutz can get it and enjoy understanding.

There are so many people who could benefit from reading *Opposites Attract*. Young couples need to read it as a prerequisite of premarital counseling. Others who are already deep into the process of discovering that their handsome prince is not always a prince, or that their beautiful sweet princess is anything but, need to read it until they can laugh at themselves and discover healing ways in our Lord that make our less-than-we-thought marriage into the better-than-we-hoped blessing that God intended from the beginning.

Yet the wisdom and insights here ought not to be boxed in as though only for engaged or married couples. Carl is using marriage problems as the understandable springboard we can all identify with (if married, or through our life with our parents) to take us into the more general process of being redeemed and transformed into the character of our Lord. The wisdom can be applied to all of life. Which is to say: *If you are not yet married, or maybe never will be, you will still find help and humor for all of life here anyway.*

So many times these days waitresses and waiters say, "Enjoy," that I can't help feeling guilty if I don't! You won't have to struggle with that when you read this book. So I say to you, "Enjoy!" It's okay to be happy. God wants you to. Read, so that joy can permeate your life and marriage.

John Sandford
Elijah House Ministries

Preface

Ever hear the joke about the doctor who "practices medicine"? Admittedly, much of what we learn about life and ministry is through the process of trial and error. Most of what Karen and I have come to understand has come through this sometimes painful but always impacting process.

I often think back to my early years of ministry when all I knew was theory—oh, the poor souls who endured my maturation. I am so grateful to the Body of Christ who has patiently listened and supported me while I tried to gather wisdom. I shudder when I think back at some of the sermons I have preached with great conviction but with little experience. I prayerfully hope that the couples I counseled early on somehow survived my zeal and were sustained by the Lord. Praise God for all the precious sheep who have faithfully followed as I have tried to learn the shepherding skills needed to lead the flock and teach them God's ways.

God's love is an amazing thing! The Bible tells us that it "knits us together." What a beautiful picture of lives intertwined with a strength and warmth that comes from that unity.

I am so blessed to have been surrounded by such wonderful and supportive friends and loved ones who have let me "practice" on them.

Most of all I am eternally thankful for God's grace, His undeserved favor! His grace has covered our lives and sheltered us in the darkest of storms and in the times when hope's light in our ministry and our marriage seemed to be fading. His grace truly is sufficient for us!

Introduction

I t is an unexplainable force in physics: "opposites attract." In magnets, electrons, or people, just look at the world around us and you can see it everywhere. The Bible tells us that God sustains the universe and everything in it (see Heb. 1:3); and in His grand plan, God has set in motion this phenomenon of opposite characteristics and natures being drawn together. Somehow it seems to hold the universe itself in balance.

The following scene has repeated itself dozens of times in my office. Two young (or even not so young) people sit down, and we begin their premarital counseling sessions. However, judging by their response, I might as well be speaking a foreign language. They look at each other with silly grins on their faces, nodding at appropriate times, but obviously not a word is penetrating their hearts.

"Marriage is hard work," I tell them. "Things that you find so endearing right now are going to drive you crazy in just a few months or even weeks. Marriage means dying to your own ways and becoming a servant to the other."

"Oh, but Pastor Carl, we are in love. I know other couples may have these problems, but we have something special and wonderful."

Now, ask anyone who knows me, and they will tell you that I am one of the world's foremost optimists. I can be down 20-to-1 in a racquetball game yet still be sure that I am going to win. I have told my wife that I am so much of an optimist that even my blood type is "B positive." But as I sit there in those types of counseling sessions, I think, *I will see you two back here in a year or two, certain that your world is over. You'll be sitting in the same seats then, certain that some alien force has taken your Prince Charming and your Cinderella and turned them into toads.*

Admittedly, Karen and I were no different. I distinctly remember driving across Arizona and listening to a "marriage veteran" on a cassette tape warning of the soon-to-come "awakening." We, like millions of couples before us, looked at each other with a sweet smile, squeezed hands, and thought, *Those poor souls.*

The "awakening." That describes it, doesn't it? As if someone pulls a blindfold off your eyes, and suddenly you're aware of something you had no idea about before. *Wait just a minute! you think. What is going on? Who are **you**, and what are you doing in my wife's dress?*

Our "awakening" began within a few hours of our "I do's." For Karen, I believe it started as we opened our wedding gifts: three Coleman camp stoves and several beautiful new ice chests. *Is this some kind of joke?* she thought. *What on earth would you use these for, and who would give such a gift?* To make matters worse, my eyes were twinkling at the sight of shiny new stoves with no year-old pancake batter welded on them. Karen looked at me with that "What's going on?" look, followed by the sickly "What have I done?" look.

You see, I am a nature boy! I grew up camping and fishing, gutting game, and sleeping on the ground under the stars. In biology in high school, I would amaze my classmates as I could dissect in record time the various preserved animals brought before us, naming all the internal parts. Some of my hunting buddies had affectionately named me "Dirt Man" because of my "Why bother to clean the pot? It will get used again tomorrow" attitude.

In contrast, Karen's one and only outdoor experience was at Fred's Lake—one of those "pay a quarter per inch" ponds full of hand-fed trout. Now you have to understand, for as long as I can remember, anytime I drove by places like that I would laugh at those "greenhorn city slickers" as I traveled to a *real* lake to catch *real* fish. Little did I know that I would marry one of those "greenhorns" disguised as my princess. I had envisioned her in a beautiful set of waders with matching vest, her lovely strawberry-blond hair gently rippling in the breeze, as she blew me a kiss while making the picture-perfect cast with her custom fly rod.

For me, the awakening began this way. My friends had a tradition of chasing the bride and groom out of the parking lot as they left the church and following them as far as possible, delaying the long-awaited honeymoon. I had been a part of some classic chases in my day and had tormented many couples. Therefore, being the brilliant strategist that I am, I planned carefully for the glorious day. While my lovely bride worked on flowers and dresses, décor and cakes, I masterminded a brilliant escape route: Just yards from the church parking lot was a dirt trail that would be our way to freedom.

Finally the big day arrived. We ran out past the showers of rice to my 1969 Dodge pickup. It was, of course, covered with shaving cream and "JUST MARRIED" slogans. The cab was full of Cracker Jacks, which, incidentally, don't do well on upholstery in the August Arizona sun. The steering wheel was covered with some poor wife's lipstick, and a line of cars anxiously waited for the green flag, like the starting of the Indy 500. I wiped off enough lipstick, so I could hold on to the wheel, and away we sped. Out of the parking lot we went, flying down the dirt path that declined sharply into a desert wash. Truck bouncing and stuff flying, I knew that few, if any, could follow my short-bed Dodge. (I found out later that my best man, who was first in line behind me, lost his muffler on that wash, blocking the would-be pursuers.)

Now, this is fun! I thought. *It doesn't get any better than this!* I was overjoyed at my brilliant plan, certain that my new bride must be amazed with the clever man she had just married. Looking over at her, I expected to see adoration, but her eyes were full of tears. Months of planning, a beautiful ceremony, hours of pictures, a piece of wedding cake and punch not a good idea for someone with low blood sugar, and a roller-coaster ride (Karen still hates to be jostled) to start the honeymoon had all overwhelmed her. Then followed the first of about 100,000 times that I would ask that famous, yet still unproductive, question: "Is something wrong?" And she responded with the first of about 100,000 answers, which I barely heard over the sobs, "No, nothing."

Thus began our "awakening." How had we not seen it before? How had we been so blind to something so obvious? She is sanguine/melancholic; I am phlegmatic/choleric (for those of you who study temperaments). She is either bouncing off the ceiling with joy or in the pit of despair; I am a right-down-the-middle kind of guy—Mister Steady. I like sports; she likes Broadway. I like country life; she likes the city. I tend to be overconfident; she always questions her ability. I could go on and on.

What kind of cruel trick had God played on us? We were absolutely sure that He had brought us together—solid and mature (so we thought) Christians who had prayed for years for God's choice in a mate. Pastors had confirmed our union, and friends had rejoiced. I remember one teacher at the Bible college where we met telling me that he could see God had given each of us His best in the other. At the wedding, God's presence had been powerful, and our parents wholeheartedly blessed our marriage. Now suddenly as the awaking occurred, we began to see our many differences. Some say that incompatibility is grounds for divorce. If that were the case, I am sure that no judge in the country would have refused us (if we believed that)!

With God, all things are possible...

Just a few evenings ago, now almost 25 years down the road, Karen and I sat in a friend's living room and counseled two couples in crisis. As has happened many times before, the Holy Spirit directed us in helping them sort things out, and God just touched them—that's all I can say. It was a joy to behold, and both Karen and I rejoiced with them as they wept with tears of happiness. I was able to share some practical scriptural principles that brought them to repentance and freedom. Karen (so very sensitive to the Holy Spirit) spoke words that went right to the core of their being and brought healing and hope. At the close of the evening, one of the women said this to us: "You two make such a great team." Just thinking about it now makes my heart smile. Those seven little words thumb their nose at the enemy who, I am certain, thought he had us on the ropes at least a thousand times.

In the following chapters is the story that has taken place between the church parking lot where we were married and that God-filled living room. In that time period, there have been many tears, out-and-out fights, frustration, peace treaties, negotiations, anger, and sleepless nights, as well as broken promises, a secret hope that the Lord would take the other home a little early, prayers and more prayers, countless counseling sessions, books, seminars, guilt, pain—and the wonderful hand of God. By His grace, and His grace alone, we *have* become a team. Let the heavens rejoice and the earth be glad; I agree with David. There is a God, and He is good!

Over the past several years, I have watched us develop into a God-honoring, well-coordinated team that not only accepts the other's gifts and nature, but has come to value and rejoice in them. We have learned to yield to each other at appropriate times and allow God to flow through us (at least more often).

"Wait a minute," some of you might be thinking. *"Are you saying that it has taken you more than 20 years to learn to work together as a team?"*

I would love to tell you that it hasn't taken us that long but, what can I say? We are both very bull-headed. Don't get me wrong; there were many bright spots over the years, but the real teamwork has just been a long time coming. Hey, it took Moses 40 years to get ready on the backside of the wilderness, so we feel like we are ahead of the game.

The road was hard, and the way was rough. I would never have chosen it, nor would I have counseled anyone else to, but it is simply God's way. He knows just the right tool we each need to refine us and shape us into the vessel He needs. He uses an intimate tool, one so close that it can take off those rough edges—and we cannot run away from it. Or we had better not run! Karen has taken me to depths that I never would have gone on my own—ones I didn't even know existed! I have dragged her on roller coasters of adventure that are a joy for me but spelled certain death for her.

There may be many reading this book who can relate to this dilemma. You may be at the place where you'd rather kill your spouse than kiss them. *Hang in there! God is at work!* Maybe you have even come up with "really good" justifications, reasons why you can't continue:

- "We were not Christians when we got married."
- "My situation is different and special."
- "I don't think God wants me to be so unhappy."
- "I married in rebellion, so I need to dump this guy or girl, repent, and start over."

I have heard those excuses for years, and this is my response: Is God in control or not? Do *all things work together for the good of those who love God and are called according to His purposes*—as it says in Romans 8:28—or not? Some of us would like to rewrite that verse to say that all things work together for good, except for my wife/husband. The Greek word translated as "all" in that verse is *pan*. It means all, any, everything. Sorry, no way out for you there!

I want to encourage you to stop trying to find a loophole and embrace the hand of God. If God can take Karen and me, possibly the two most opposite people on Planet Earth, and blend us together to be a "great team," then He can surely do it for you!

I believe with all my heart that this opposite attraction thing is an incredible gift to us. It just doesn't seem like it at first. In Genesis 2:18 (NLT), God says, *"It is not good for the man to be alone. I will make a helper who is just right for him."* I have heard this word "helper" also translated as "completer." What do you need to complete a jigsaw puzzle? The pieces that are missing. When God handpicks our mate, He chooses someone with pieces different from ours. If He gave us someone just like ourself, the picture would not be complete. Our job is to let Him fit us together. This takes patience, yielded hearts, and faith.

Not all couples have the extremes of natures that Karen and I have. They may have similar gifts and design. They are different puzzles for a different purpose. Just as God creates each person on the face of the earth for a unique purpose, so each couple or team is created for His great purpose and plan. Some seem to fit together easier, and they don't have to go through the intensity of finding balance as Karen and I have did; some may deal with even more differences than us (though that's hard for me to imagine). To both ends of this spectrum I say, "Be who God created you to be. Resist the temptation to compare yourselves to other couples." Paul said it this way in his second letter to the couples in Corinth: *"When they measure themselves by themselves and compare themselves with themselves, they are not wise"* (2 Cor. 10:12 NIV).

Remember as kids when we discovered the magic of magnets? I would sneak them to school and entertain myself for hours, when I should have been paying attention to the English teacher. Opposite poles attract. It is still a mystery to me how God designs things in such a way. Over the years, I have come to understand, through acquired wisdom (and sometimes sheer exhaustion), that God really does know what He is doing. He will take people extremely contrary in nature and use their opposite qualities to balance and bind them together in a powerful way. We just need to be patient and trust God to make it work.

CHAPTER 1

A Hawk Marrying a Turtle?

About two years ago, a key couple in our church came to Karen and me for some counsel. They were struggling with some issues, and their involvement in ministry had really forced things to the surface. We could relate so well as they described their frustration of trying to minister together, while being so very different in gifts, temperament, and almost every other way. (To respect their privacy, we'll call them "Jack" and "Jill.")

Jill was the one who loved to soar with spiritual wings. Motivated and gifted with that pioneering spirit, she was always pressing forward into new territories in life and ministry. If she had been born 100 years earlier, I am sure she would have been a wagon-train master. I can see her sitting proudly on her buck-skin steed ready to lead the band of adventurers to parts unknown. Jill would have given each family an itinerary and then color-coded the wagons. Organized, administrative, first-born, type A, a natural leader and self-confident to a fault, her T-shirt would have read, "Get In, Get Out, or Get Run Over!"

Her husband, Jack, was just the opposite in about every way. Life is much more of a struggle for him. Many of his goals and dreams have been stolen by fears and uncertainty. While Jill loves to be up front and in control, Jack has a tendency to freeze under pressure. More a servant than a leader, a "focus on one thing at a time" kind of guy, he's very sensitive—except when it comes to Jill—and he struggles with his confidence and purpose for life. I doubt very seriously that you would find Jack on a wagon train. He would believe that such a venture would lead to certain and painful death. Kind, compassionate, and ready at a moment's notice to serve those in need, Jack always seemed to be at opposite ends of the spectrum from Jill.

Karen and I sat and listened to them share their frustrations and resentments toward each other. They had been married for many years, had raised a family and "coped"—sometimes well, sometimes not so well—with the tension caused by their differences. Years of hurt and pain, trying to understand and praying for grace, had brought them to where they were willing to be vulnerable enough to get some assistance. It is the place Karen says has become one of our best friends: "Desperation." In a moment of unusual spiritual brilliance, I suggested that we pray. (I sometimes resort to that when I don't have a clue what to do.)

Shortly after we began to pray, I heard these very unusual and shocking words flood into my heart: *"This is what happens when a hawk marries a turtle."*

Now after 20 years of ministry, I hope that I have learned (at least sometimes) to discern the voice of the Lord. When a thought comes to me that I know wasn't by way of my normal conscious logic, it is often the Lord. In this instance, I wasn't trying to come up with an idea of what Jill and Jack were like and then matching an animal to each of them. The comparison was just suddenly there.

Wow, I thought, *that really describes them!* After some time in prayer, I submitted to them the phrase that had come to me. They both felt the picture accurately expressed the frustration they had experienced.

For Jill, it revealed years of feeling held back and restricted her wings clipped and feet tied down—and not understanding why. Frustration turned to resentment toward Jack and probably God as well. For Jack, it was the feeling of incompetence and always being left behind, as well the fear of Jill's flying off someday and not returning. *Was the marriage a mistake?*

I am sure that thought had crossed their minds hundreds of times. God wouldn't think of tying two such unlikely critters together, would He? It brought all sorts of conflict into their world. Turtles, though cute and approachable, seem to move too slowly, have a shell that's too hard and a far too limited view of the world to be leaders and give direction. When Jill was in the lead it seemed so much easier, so that's where they went. Yet, the Scriptures instruct a wife to respect her husband and submit to his leadership. How was Jill to be faithful to God's Word and at the same time be the person He had created her to be? It didn't seem fair. "I don't want to be married to a turtle! I want another hawk, or an eagle; I'll even take a buzzard—anything that can fly." Although Jill never actually said the "buzzard" part, I believe she was thinking it.

For Jack, the dilemma was just as acute. "Well, it is not so wonderful to be married to a hawk, you know. She's always on the verge of being out of sight." He was never sure she would return from her journeys to spiritual lands unknown to him. Try as he might, there was no way to keep up with her. He was full of frustration and anger directed at her (though it was mostly about himself). The answer for Jack was to tie her down, clip her wings, and keep her on the ground. For Jill, the solution was to teach *him* to fly!

In my early life, I loved to backpack and hike. (I still love it; I just don't love it as often.) On several occasions I had hiked to the bottom of the Grand Canyon. I had explored many of the trails there and, though all were very physically challenging, discovered that the reward for such grueling effort was unparalleled beauty. After marriage, Karen listened intently as I would recount my adventures. She heard all the stories of muscle cramps and blisters, 50-pound packs and freezing temperatures, and grown men, sitting and crying by the sides of the trail as they climbed the 5,000 vertical feet in the 7.2-mile hike out. She heard about icy paths on our winter hikes and fatigue beyond what seemed bearable.

I tried to convince her that this would be fun! "We can share it together!" Then I told her about a couple who had hiked it on their anniversaries all the way to the 50th. Finally, during one of my attempts to lure her on a trip, she took my face in her hands like a mother with a distracted three-year-old. Pulling me close, she said these wise words I shall never forget: "If I go with you to the bottom of the Grand Canyon, I guarantee you that neither one of us will have fun!" That was the last time I asked.

Now here is an important piece of wisdom: Trying to force our spouse to live in our world and be like us often has an adverse effect. Although we might think it would be fun if our spouse enjoyed everything we enjoy, "fun" is not our ultimate aim—giving glory to God is. Allowing our partner to be who God created them to be does just that. It was not fun or fruitful for Jill to be tied to the ground and forced to move about at the turtle's pace; nor is it fun to be urged to fly when you are not equipped with wings. Yet many of us, wanting to become that "one flesh" that the Bible talks about, try to make our partner live our lives.

Now don't get me wrong: Karen and I have found common ground, and there are many things that we have fun doing together. In any successful relationship, self-sacrifice is appropriate and commanded in the Word. Giving up or compromising some of our ways for our mate is important, but don't ask your husband or wife to change their God-ordained characteristics just for your own comfort.

For example, I try hard to be interested and enthused on shopping trips, and I have attended my share of plays and performances. Karen has tolerated several camping trips and has even reeled in a few fish. However, God did not design her to love pushing herself to exhaustion on a mountain trail or gutting a bear for hours after dark. Nor has He made me to have that ultra-sensitivity to people's emotional wounds that Karen came equipped with. Over the years, we have learned to discern what things are to be compromised for the sake of the relationship and what things are put there by God and not intended to be changed.

There are several important Kingdom principles to be learned here. *First, we must learn to value the God-designed traits in our mate as well as in ourselves.*

It is funny how we humans identify ourselves with the animal kingdom. We pick out animals with certain traits and use them to describe the nature and character of people. For instance, we've all heard expressions such as: "He's as strong as an ox" or "busy as a beaver," or how about "old eagle eye"? I remember as a young man going for a job interview. The committee doing the interview asked an unusual final question: "What kind of an animal would you say you are most like and why?" I was a little stunned by the question, and my mind raced to try to figure out the right response. I decided at first that I was a lion. Yes, that's it, agile, fearless, king of the beasts. But I had to pause; they are also ruthless killers! No, that wasn't going to work. Then I thought, *Maybe I'm a dolphin. They are playful, intelligent, and they look like they are always smiling.* Almost too late, I remembered that they play around too much. I scanned my memory banks for good candidates. Sloth? No. Rattlesnake? No. Turkey? Well, maybe, if I were going to be honest, but no! Duck-billed platypus? (Where did that come from?) No!

I finally got it: "I'm a bear!" Confident, powerful, yet not obnoxious. They know who they are and are not afraid of anything. I was sure that I had picked the perfect animal to represent what they were looking for. Then just about the time I reached the door it hit me: *Wait a minute! They take four months off every winter and do nothing but sleep.* Apparently the committee knew a little about bears too, since I never heard from them again.

Here is my point. Although all these animals are created by God with unique and wonderful characteristics, we tend to classify them as "good" and "not so good." I am quite sure that anyone who gave "turtle" as the answer to the committee's question would not fare well. "Peaceful, patient, kind, and gentle" certainly describe the turtle, and they also happen to be some of the fruits of the spirit listed in Galatians 5. The things God values are often not valued by the world or even by the church. There is not a more approachable animal in all of creation than the turtle. Except for the ornery snapping turtle, most turtles seem to invite you to come and enjoy them. Even the giant tortoises of the Galapagos Islands do not inspire fear in children. Turtles see things that hawks will never see from their lofty heights. They are able to connect with people who would never go near a hawk; hawks are too scary—remember, they eat cute, little, furry woodland creatures for lunch. The turtle's gentle disposition and slow movements are endearing and, in many ways, "Christlike."

Second, in learning to value what God values, we have to look at our own sinful responses and attitudes. Jack and Jill had some repenting to do. In Jill's mind, it was obvious that the hawk was the "right" animal, and if Jack would just get his act together and get healed, he would learn to soar with her. Hawk good, turtle bad. The Bible calls this attitude "pride," and pride is never a good thing, as we see in Proverbs 16:18: *"**Pride** goes before **destruction**, and a **haughty spirit** before a **fall**."* When you are a hawk, that can mean falling a long way.

In the months following our counseling session, Jill began to change her mind about turtles and hawks. Their many differences still posed some unique challenges, but agreeing with God—realizing that both turtles and hawks are acceptable, and even God-designed, and that *both* have strengths and weaknesses—was a start.

For Jack, the problem was not pride. It was anger and frustration with the characteristics the Lord had chosen for him. Not accepting the way God has made us for His purposes is a form of rebellion. First Samuel 15:23 says that *"rebellion is as the sin of witchcraft."* Wow! That is pretty serious in the scope of things. This means changing your mind from, "I got the short end of the stick," to thanking God for His choices for us. That is easier said than done, I know. But so are most of the things the Bible tells us to do.

Repenting of our sinful attitudes is always a fruitful beginning. Paul, in his second letter to the church at Corinth, said it this way, *"Godly sorrow produces repentance"* (2 Cor. 7:10a). In other words, repentance is a change of heart and mind that leads to a change of behavior. Too often, we have had sorrow because we are not getting along with one another or we are not happy in our marriage; but that's not a *godly sorrow*. Godly sorrow comes when we realize that we have grieved the heart of God because of pride about ourselves, or because we have not accepted with gratefulness the person God has created us to be.

To quote Jill, "As I have looked at this, some very ugly attitudes I didn't even know were there have come out of me." Aha! Now we are getting to one of the primary reasons I believe God hooks us up with, shall we say, "strange bedfellows." It is one of the many loving ways He brings our sin to the surface in our lives. If Jill had married another hawk, she might still be soaring from one spiritual high to the next without realizing the pride that was lodged in her heart. If Jack had married another turtle, he might still be walking around with his rebellion towards God not revealed.

Let this next statement sink in, as it is probably the most important point I hope to make in this book: *God is more interested in our being right with Him than He is in our being happy in our marriages!* Being "right" with Him means getting our sin to the surface where it can be repented of.

The *third principle* to look at here is that *marriage is God's way of getting us ready to bring the true light and hope of Christ to the world.* It is one of the tools He uses to purify us and shine us up, so we reflect Him accurately. In other words, there is a much greater purpose in our marriages than just being happy and blessing each other. It is a Kingdom purpose. I tell those who come for premarital counsel that the first and foremost reason for marriage is that together they can be more effective for God's Kingdom than they were as individuals.

It is often through the struggles and intimacy that God does His deepest work in our individual hearts—to prepare us for His divine plan. In Second Corinthians 5:18b-20 (NLT), Paul says it this way:

> *God has given us the task of reconciling people to Him. For God was in Christ, reconciling the world to Himself, no longer counting people's sins against them. This is the wonderful message He has given us to tell others. We are Christ's ambassadors, and God is using us to speak to you. We urge you, as though Christ Himself were here pleading with you, "Be reconciled to God!"*

Why is Christ pleading with us to be reconciled to God? So we will be better ambassadors of His wonderful message. We cannot be good reconcilers until *we* have been reconciled.

Look at it this way: When God hitches a hawk and a turtle together, ambassador training. *"Reconciliation"* means to restore.

People all around us need to be restored to a right relationship with God, which comes only through knowing Christ and His forgiveness of our sins. Reconciliation is bridge-building. We have to have *our* bridge in good shape before we can even reach others to restore theirs. At least in Karen's and my life, as well as the lives of Jack and Jill, marriage has been a wonderful "bridge inspector." It has revealed weak and sinful areas none of us were aware of, attitudes and actions that need repentance.

Most marriage counseling I have done starts out with both parties pointing the finger at the other. "If he (or she) would just change, we would not be having these difficulties." I have found that, in God's economy, He wastes nothing. By that, I mean that He handpicks a mate who will be just the right "tool" we need to shape us into the ambassador He has destined us to become. I have heard of couples divorcing because of "irreconcilable differences." Yet it is very often those differences that make us better reconcilers.

Whether hawk or turtle, horse or lizard, listen to what David says about our inner character and our creation. Psalm 139:13-14 (NIV) says, *"For You created my inmost being; You knit me together in my mother's womb. I praise You because I am fearfully* [reverently] *and wonderfully made; Your works are wonderful, I know that full well."* Do you know that full well? Do you believe it not only in your head but in your heart? God's Word proclaims it, and it is true. No matter how limited or how un-wonderful you feel, you are God's handiwork created for His purposes; and His purposes often involve teaming up turtles with hawks and the like. To torment them? No, to make teams that can utilize the qualities of each individual for God's glory.

You may be wondering: Are Jack and Jill, the turtle and the hawk, now perfectly synchronized in their ministry and lives together? Not yet! But they are getting there.

CHAPTER 2

Flying Lessons

K aren and I sat patiently waiting in the beautiful new 757 jet. The two-hour delay had given us plenty of time to survey the busy Los Angeles International airport. Bright-colored giants took off and landed every 20-30 seconds, and finally, it was our turn. Carrying 190 passengers, a crew of 14, and thousands of pounds of fuel, luggage, and miscellaneous stuff, our plane started down the concrete runway. After reaching the proper speed, the plane lifted off the runway and powered its way into the wild blue yonder.

I have flown to four continents, over many oceans, and yet flying still amazes me. Many years ago, a couple of really determined brothers experimented with the concepts of lift, drag, thrust, and weight (the four forces of flight)...and it changed our lives forever. These modern miracles are designed to fly— and fly they do. As we soared eastward, I watched the intricately fashioned wing parts move as directed, giving perfect control to the pilots at the helm. Planes are not made to drive on freeways, nor are they designed to speed across the surface of the oceans. They are created to fly! Try to use them for any other purpose, and it simply will not work.

I have sat on hundreds of hillsides and watched this in Nature's realm. Beautifully, effortlessly, riding the air currents, rarely wasting the energy to flap the God-designed master-pieces called wings—hawks, eagles, ospreys, and falcons all fas-cinate me. As magnificent birds of prey, they circle the sky, scanning the landscape for the smallest movement below. Powerful and perfectly formed by the Creator, every feather is in its place, and each is carefully designed. The red-tailed hawk rises to a perch high above the forest floor. She gently lands on the very top branch, and her powerful talons get a good grip. She sits like a statue, with her head turning slightly to search for food. Suddenly and without warning, she plunges off the branch and goes straight into her dive, wings folded for maxi-mum speed. The unsuspecting ground squirrel never sees her coming, and it is over quickly. The hawk wings her way back home with supper for her waiting brood. Like the jets, she is designed to fly—and fly she does. Graceful and dynamic in the air, hawks are awkward on the ground. Make them walk, and they are like fish out of water.

Picture this, if you will: the hawk and the turtle joined in marriage (as in Chapter 1). The "I do's" are all said, and the happy couple settles in for a joy-filled life together. The hawk's "awakening" comes suddenly. How could she have missed something so important? The turtle can't fly! During their courtship, she had assumed that he simply *chose* not to fly. Now, however, they are going forward together, and to her, flying is necessary. It's a natural part of life that takes little effort, and she is sure that he just hasn't been given the chance to try. From the turtle's perspective, he had assumed that once they started their life together she would give up this foolishness of taking off and going here and there. He just knew the hawk would be content to walk patiently down the path God had chosen for them.

Here is the scene: The hawk gently encourages her mate closer and closer to the 50-foot drop-off. Wanting to please her, the turtle slowly stretches out his neck to peer over the edge. Beads of perspiration appear on his forehead, and the sight of the rocks below causes him instinctively to pull back into the safety of his shell. Love and encouragement from his mate draws him out again to the edge. He nervously looks at the makeshift wings strapped to his stubby little legs. At her direction, he moves them awkwardly back and forth. Several times, she leaps off the cliff, demonstrates the principles of flight, and circles back to his side. It seems so easy and natural to her, and she is growing impatient with the many "how do I" and "what if" questions and the time it is taking him to move to action. She takes off again and this time remains aloft several feet from the edge. "Flap faster!" she instructs. Unfortunately, his muscular legs don't do "fast."

Love propels him forward, and he lunges off the overhanging cliff. For one very brief moment, there is excitement in their eyes as they meet in the air. But that excitement is followed by a look of sheer terror as he suddenly plunges downward, like a kite with an anvil attached to it. He slams into the rocks below and comes to rest on his back. The hawk dives to his side and gently turns him upright. Bruised and stunned, a look of failure and disappointment now fills his eyes. At her encouragement, he reluctantly climbs the hillside again, and the scene repeats itself. Any confidence he had is quickly eroded with each attempt. His fear is followed by anger, then resentment.

Now, her instruction turns to accusation. "You don't really want to fly," she barks. "If you did, you'd just make up your mind and do it!"

The turtle replies, "You don't understand. I *can't* fly, and if you really loved me, you wouldn't fly either."

After watching him plummet time after time (and having compassion for her mate), the hawk feels compelled to ground herself. Now, it is the turtle's turn to demonstrate how to walk through life. The hawk watches patiently as he slowly puts one foot in front of the other. "You will eventually get there," he instructs, and he recalls for her every turtle's favorite story, the Tortoise and the Hare! The hawk walks slowly behind, held down by love, and tries to remain patient. The turtle shows her how to do the only thing he can do quickly: pull back into the safety of his shell. She tries, but it just doesn't work. On they go, torn between the love that brought them together in the first place and the frustration of doing what seems so unnatural. Sometimes they experience compassion for the struggles of the other; but sometimes they just feel angry at their spouse or even at God for putting them together. The "if only" thoughts become more and more frequent. Their emotions bounce from acceptance of God's plan to "I can't live my life this way."

Over and over, it happens on different ledges and different pathways. He keeps trying the occasional jump, to please her; and she walks with him, since he can't (or won't) fly, but both resent it deeply.

Let me take this to real life. It was a joyful day at one of the theme parks in the southern California area. Karen and I had taken our youngest son, ten years old at the time, for his first visit. After 23 years of marriage, although I have come to value her strengths and qualities and we have learned to work as a God-created team, sometimes I still forget some of the lessons God has taught us. I tend to be more hawk-like and Karen more turtle-like. It took me most of the day, but finally I had coaxed them into a line for one of the tamer roller coasters. Remember, Karen does not like to be jostled! She gets sick to her stomach, afraid, and then angry. For her, hell would be a roller coaster ride that never ends.

"Just make up your mind that you are going to enjoy it," I encouraged. Sound familiar?

Love, and a desire not to disappoint me, propelled her all the way to the front of the line, where there was a huge sign with big red letters: "WARNING! If you have a heart condition, back problems, are pregnant, elderly, or are a chicken (I added that part), DO NOT GO ON THIS RIDE!" That was it for Karen. Here we were supposed to be enjoying a wonderful day together, and I had my wife near tears wanting her to "take the leap." It finally dawned on me that I had regressed and fallen into the old pattern again.

Suddenly it occurred to me that her reluctance to go on the roller coaster did not mean that she didn't love me or that she did not want to be with me—she just doesn't fly in those areas. At the core of her being, the thrill and excitement of the ride, being jostled and tossed about (whether at the park or in life), is not a joy. On the other hand, I love adventure! I am forever jumping off cliffs and figuring out how to fly on the way down. It is just who God made me. It is the spice of my life. Some of us like jalapeños and, for others, plain old salt is just fine. One is not right and the other wrong. So I went on the ride by myself, and Karen and my son met me at the exit. Everyone was happy!

Lurking behind the attempts to re-train our spouses to take on our nature is often a deep-seated fear of being left by the one we love. For the turtle, it's the feeling that someday the hawk will fly off and not return. She may get caught up in the heights and forget about him altogether. She might meet another hawk, and then how could he possibly compete? So, at his request, she clips her wings. For the hawk, it can be the fear that the turtle will withdraw into the shell, never to re-emerge. She would be left alone.

Fear is a powerful motivator. It can even override love. For example, Peter loved Jesus intensely. Yet when He needed him most, fear caused Peter to deny that he knew Him. Fear of losing our mates can cause us to do things like trying to make them be like us. In the long run, it can have the very effect we are trying to avoid: pushing them away. Jesus said it this way. *"If you try to keep your life* [or mate]...*you will lose it. But if you give up your life* [let them be who they were created to be] *for My sake...you will find true life"* (Mark 8:35 NLT). Interestingly enough, in nature both the hawk and turtle have nests that they always return to.

I want to try to bring this struggle into the world of our ministry. God has designed me to love preparing sermons, to study and share the Word with anyone who will listen. Every Sunday, I am at the church early to prepare my heart and to review my sermon. Sometimes I get so excited to tell what God has given me, I feel like calling the congregation to come early. I am ready to preach! So what if it's 6:30 a.m.? I have a "Word from the Lord"! However, better judgment prevails, and I wait until the appointed time. As a young man, I got nervous like everyone else, but that soon gave way to the joy of speaking and teaching the Lord's Word. I am reminded of the Academy Award-winning film, *Chariots of Fire*, based on the real-life story of the gold medalist Eric Liddell. In the movie, he said of his running, "God has made me fast, and when I run I feel His pleasure." When I am preparing and teaching the Word of God, I feel God's pleasure.

For Karen, the pressure of teaching a prepared lesson is overwhelming. She will lie awake night after night and fret. She tries praying, studying, and practicing, but she mostly just panics. Karen loves the Word and is a great communicator, but the responsibility of being the key leader usually overwhelms her. She cannot "fly" with it no matter how hard she tries. For years, I encouraged her to face her fears and just "do it." It was like strapping wings on the turtle. She simply was not created for this purpose. Now when I have prepared a lesson and have the responsibility to be the leader, she often will freely share incredible insights, sometimes for the majority of the time. I just start the class and sit back in amazement as Karen is used by God in wonderful ways. But put her in charge, and she freezes. I tried to change her, which (believe me) just about killed both of us, but I can now accept her God-given design and rejoice in it. I can press her to be like me, or I can bless and encourage the uniqueness of who she is.

Remember Jack and Jill? They experienced much the same struggles as Karen and I have. Early on in their marriage, they both worked in retail with different companies. Jill, just being herself, would quickly rise in management levels and salary. Jack continued along faithfully, but the stable company he worked for offered little advancement. Jack became fearful that

Jill would leave him in the dust as she moved upward. The higher she flew, the more intense his fear and the stronger his attempts to ground her. Interestingly enough, it also showed up in their attempts to work together in ministry. They often would prepare to co-teach the classes. Jill would share her part clearly and freely. When it was Jack's turn, his struggle was obvious. He is a very sensitive guy, intelligent and gifted in many ways. There is not a more respected and loved man in our church. Yet teaching in front of a group is just not his forte. Jill would try to rescue him, which would end up causing Jack to feel stupid and incapable.

I have been to at least a hundred classes, sermons, and teachings on marriage and ministry. Both subtly (and not so subtly) the message has been sent: "If you have a truly godly marriage, you will find a way to minister together." I do believe the primary reason for marriage is that together we can be far more effective for God's Kingdom than we can alone. Unfortunately, this has been translated by many to "strap the wings" on our mates and make them be like us. I remember the Nike commercial with the slogan "be like Mike." It used the famous star from the Chicago Bulls, Michael Jordan, to sell basketball shoes. The commercials showed Michael performing some of his spectacular moves, and the message was that if you buy the shoes you can "be like Mike." I love basketball and I even have his shoes, but my jump shot just does not look like his. I will never, this side of heaven, do a 360-degree slam-dunk on a full-size hoop (without the aid of a trampoline).

As Karen and I have learned these lessons over the years, we have seen the dangers and pitfalls of not accepting God's design and plan for each of us. I no longer want her to be like me. If God needed another "me," He certainly could have handled that. I now encourage Karen to be herself: that wonderful creation God designed, planned, and spoke into existence, then blessed me with as a wife. I have said to her, "Just because you happen to be the pastor's wife, doesn't mean that you have to be 'the pastor's wife,'" if you know what I mean. We put expectations on people to be what we think they ought to be—in reality, telling them not to become the person *God* created. "Pastors' wives" often have certain expectations put on them, and Karen simply does not fit into that mold. Gratefully, I pastor a church that loves and accepts Karen as Karen! They give her the freedom to be herself, and I believe she feels God's pleasure, as do I. If God wanted turtles to fly, He would have given them wings!

But ask the animals, and they will teach you, or the birds of the air, and they will tell you! (Job 12:7 **NIV**)

CHAPTER 3

When Turtles Soar!

There is something endearing about the quiet nature of a turtle. I was fascinated by them when I was a child. I would spend hours trying to find one. Many of you may have had a turtle as a pet. My early years were spent in the Midwest where the box turtles were plentiful. I remember begging my father to stop the car when we saw one crossing the highway. They move slowly, don't bark, and generally do not bite. They quickly get over their fear of humans and seem to make the best of life. Children and turtles just go together.

To people with hawk-like personality types, "turtles" are often thought of in a negative light. For the most part, our world puts a much greater value on these hawk characteristics than on those of the turtle. I want to state again that the things we value in the world (and often in the church) are not usually what God values. Success in your field of employment can certainly be a good thing; being a faithful person and obeying the Scriptures should cause us to rise to the top. The Word of God states, *"Whatever you do, do it heartily, as to the Lord and not to men"* (Col. 3:23). However, the hawk-like traits I have talked about can be a hindrance in our life and our walk with God. "Hawks" tend to be self-reliant, self-motivated, self-assured, self-confident, and many other "self" things. These are not really great attributes in the Kingdom of God.

I have had to continually bring my self-reliance to the cross, especially being a pastor. Paul told the church at Rome: *"I know that in me (that is, in my flesh) nothing good dwells"* (Rom. 7:18). All of that self-stuff is formed in the flesh part of us. I can almost hear some of you right now saying, "Wait just a minute! You mean self-confidence is not a good thing?" That's right! If it is based in your ability and not in God, it will end up in pride—and God resists the proud. When we can honestly say, "If there is any good thing in me, I have God alone to thank," then we are on our way.

A pastor once gave me a definition of humility that has stayed with me over many years: "Humility is wanting to be known for who we really are and agreeing with God about our sin." Here is who I really am apart from God: a sinful, rebellious, wicked, and despicable human who deserves eternal punishment for my sins. Thanks to God's great mercy, I have been transformed into a holy, righteous son of God who can stand spotless before Him without fear because of one reason alone: Jesus took my sinfulness on Himself.

Let's return to the turtle and who God has made him. The hawk and the turtle sit together on the edge of a deep gorge. They agree that God is directing them forward. The hawk takes off, catches a rising air current and glides majestically across the mile-wide canyon to a perch on the other side. It took only minutes to cross, and she turns to see the progress of her mate. The turtle has barely begun the descent. The hawk had a grand view of the beautiful valley below as she soared overhead. She saw the meandering brook and the lush green trees and meadows. She spotted the doe with her fawn resting in the shade of a cottonwood tree. If asked, she could describe the scene quite nicely. The turtle, however, has a totally different view and experience during his trip across the gorge. His journey is long and difficult. Each little obstacle is crossed with great effort and time. What took her mere minutes will take him weeks. Slowly he goes, stopping where he can to rest and feed. The stream was nothing to her. For him, it took hours to find a shallow crossing and, even then, he was washed hundreds of feet downstream by the swift current. The trek was life-threatening to the turtle. When asked to describe the valley, his answer would be much different.

The turtle could tell you the color of the dirt and the smell of the plants. He could describe the ants and insects that inhabit the valley floor and the temperature of the stream. He could tell you about every rock and about the trees that have fallen and lie decaying on the forest floor. He too saw the doe and fawn and could describe what they looked like, but he could also tell you how it felt when he walked in their tracks and lay still while they gently nuzzled his shell, trying to figure out what he was. He saw and experienced the sights, smells, and sounds of life that go on every day in the valley. He could direct weary travelers to the freshest grasses and the coolest waters. Both hawk and turtle saw the valley—but in very different ways.

Here's an example of how this plays out in our household. Karen and I come home from another busy Sunday morning service. It amazes me every week; God once again was faithful to work and speak, even through the likes of me. People responded to the message, and everyone seemed joyful and happy to be together with their church family and especially with the Lord.

"Great service today, huh, Karen?" I kind of asked and stated at the same time.

"Yes, very nice," she replied.

I could see in her eyes, wheels were turning and something was stirring. I have learned to read my wife's eyes more than her words. So, it took me 20 years—I'm a slow learner!

"What is it?" I asked.

"John is not doing so well, and Marsha and Bill are in trouble," she replied.

"They seemed great to me when I talked to them."

"No, things are not good, and I think the nursery workers are really feeling the weight of having two services," she added.

In times past, when I was young and foolish, I would have discounted such notions as emotionalism and an overactive imagination. After all these years of her being mostly right, I have learned to listen. You see, I soared through the day. I have come to believe that God has given me this gift. If I could pick up the information Karen does, I don't believe I could deliver the message God has given me. I would be so distracted that I would have difficulty staying the course and delivering the Word. As it is though, I often have people come up to me after a service to apologize for their having to get up and leave, coughing and choking, several times during my sermon—and I hadn't even noticed, even though they were in the front row!

It is really a gift from God to me. In order to be a good shepherd, I need to be able to look over the whole flock. Karen, on the other hand, goes through that same service slowly and carefully. She observes things I would never see. She picks up the sights and smells of the flock and tells me about the lambs that are sick and in need. She senses things that were not even spoken. It is God's gift to her, to me, and to the Body of Christ.

Turtles, in my view, often devalue their specific assignment from the Almighty. Certainly, the world does. I have come to place tremendous value not only on the input from Karen but also from others in the church who are called to this. One very helpful description of this personality is a "burden bearer": someone who, by their God-given nature, has the ability to sense the heart of another person. Often, they take on the other's burden or heaviness as their own. This can happen without words being exchanged. Even secular science tells us that up to 95 percent of what we communicate is non-verbal. This can make going through a church service much more difficult for Karen than for me. It is like the two different experiences crossing the valley.

For her and others gifted in this way, it's easy to fall into self-pity and/or depression. Where pride can come easily to the hawk, self-pity is the snare of the turtle. It is another one of those "self" words. For the turtle, it seems that life has dealt them an unfair hand. Anger and resentment at God (and toward others with whom they may compare themselves) is common. Karen has often complained that it is just not fair. I breeze through things that are difficult for her and seem to take her much longer. In the long run, she experiences them much more deeply than I. As we have learned to work together (and to recognize, value, and depend upon the gifts of the other), we have seen God do some "really cool things" through and in us. As I circle overhead, I can keep us focused on the vision of our lives from the perspective God has given me. I can encourage her onward toward the goal. I have been given a platform from which to speak. Karen can give me wonderful insights from the up-close-and-personal way she sees things. She can relay to me the condition of the ones I lose sight of and the struggles of those I miss. What a team! When we are working well together as God created us, we are both in awe! I must resist the pride that can come from my soaring, and Karen must resist the self-pity of her walk through the valleys.

Self-pity is a difficult, almost overwhelming struggle for many. My heart goes out to all those who fall into this trap set by our enemy. From the natural mind's point of view, self-pity seems justified. Life doesn't appear to be fair; it seems like life is easier for one person than another.

In the Bible, Jonah was the self-pity master. He knew that God would spare the evil enemy of his people if they repented of their sin—but Jonah didn't think it was fair. Yet, sure enough, that is what happened. At the end of the story, Jonah cries out in self-pity, *"O Lord, please take my life from me, for it is better for me to die than to live!"* (Jon. 4:3). God answers with an unusual question: *"Is it right for you to be angry?"* (Jon. 4:4).

The story continues with Jonah going out to the east side of the city to see what would happen. God causes a plant to grow to provide shade for him. The next day God sends a worm to damage the plant, and it withers. Jonah is at it again: *"It is better for me to die than to live,"* he cries out. And God replies, *"Is it right for you to be angry about the plant?"* (Jon. 4:8-9).

These verses paint a vivid picture of the struggle of self-pity. Self-pity is often anger at God about His ways and plans for us. It is rooted in not understanding God's purposes. Why would God spare the evil enemy of His own people that lived in Nineveh? Why would He first bring a plant to provide shade for Jonah and then bring a worm to destroy the plant? You can hear the frustration in Jonah's response: "I don't understand You, God! What in the world are You doing? This makes no sense to me!"

As difficult as it may be, those who wrestle with self-pity must make a choice. It is a choice of faith. Psalm 18:30 states the answer in no uncertain terms: *"As for God, His way is perfect"*! The Bible also tells us that God's ways are as far above ours as the heavens are above the earth (see Isa. 55:8-9). We must come to a place of accepting that we cannot understand everything God does. That's just the way it's going to be. He is God, and we are not! We have the joy of seeing some of His purposes work out, as with Karen and me. However, this side of Heaven, there are many things we will not understand.

Comparison is a continual battle for those who struggle with self-pity. They look at the life and calling of others and feel they have been given a raw deal. "Why do they have it easy when I have it so hard?"

Jesus addressed this very issue on the seashore after His resurrection. He and Peter had been reconciled after Peter had denied Christ at His trial, and Jesus had just encouraged Peter to feed His sheep. They were walking together, and Jesus told Peter, in no uncertain terms, that he would end up giving his life as a martyr (see John 21:18-19). Peter turned and, the Bible says, he saw the "disciple that Jesus loved" following them. That would have been the apostle John, who wrote this Gospel. While Peter was getting correction, John seemed to be allowed to just soak in His love. Peter obviously was not too crazy about this "favoritism." He said to Jesus, in verse 21, *"What about this man?"* In other words, "What are You going to require of him? If I am going to have to give my life, You'd better give him something really difficult, too—it is only fair." Jesus spoke these stern words to Peter, "If I allow him to remain until I come, what is that to you? You follow Me!" (see John 21:22). That thought will nip self-pity right in the bud. Jesus was saying, "You do what I ask of you, and leave the lives of others in My charge." It is not open for discussion. If God chooses a life for others that seems easier than ours, if He gives us assignments that are just not "fair," what is that to us? We must follow the Lord!

Self-pity can also be a form of what I call "dark pride." It is kind of a hidden or masked pride. Self-pity says in effect, "I am too good to be given such a bad deal. I am better than this and don't deserve such treatment."

Often, when those in self-pity come to us and express the "unfairness," we try to encourage them and point out things they are really good at. I don't know about you, but in my experience, this rarely works or helps. The "truth" is what really sets us free, Jesus said. The truth is that you are much worse than you imagine yourself to be. You deserve a far greater punishment than anything you are experiencing now. When we agree with God about who we really are, and our sin (remember the definition of humility?), we are able to be forgiven and will not fall into self-pity. Instead, we are grateful for what God's grace and mercy have given us, even if it is "turtle traits."

It is amazing how the truth can set us free in this area. For those of you who are stuck in self-pity, try this. It really will set you free. I don't mean to be harsh concerning a difficult matter. However, the answer for this sin (yes, it is *sin*) is the same as all sin. Repent! Change your mind, and agree with God. I have learned to be wise in the way I share this with those who may find themselves trapped in self-pity, remembering always that I have my own sinful patterns to deal with. "Be wise as a serpent and gentle as a dove," the Bible tells us—and I have found this approach to be best!

Having described at length the characteristics of "hawks" and "turtles," I want to add a beautiful illustration of what happens when God gets involved. Imagine the turtle struggling through the valley. He comes to an area thick with mud. In fact, let's just do this scripturally and call it "miry clay." I love that picture. I envision "miry clay" as mud so thick and gooey that if you get into it, you can no longer pick up your feet; you become wiped out in the struggle and must cry out for help. So, our faithful turtle comes upon this area of miry clay and finds several of his friends hopelessly stuck and near the point of complete exhaustion. His mercy overrides his fear, and the little fellow comes to their rescue.

However, it is soon obvious that the turtle does not have the ability or the skill to free them in his own strength. To make matters worse, *he* is now caught in the muck! In desperation, he cries out to God. Suddenly, something strange and wonderful, something supernatural happens. Out of the hard shell on his back appear the most beautiful and powerful eagle's wings. The turtle's look of despair turns to pure joy. He lifts his friends, one at a time, out of the clay and carries them to the top edge of the valley. As he puts the last little turtle gently down, the wings disappear as quickly as they came. *"My grace is sufficient for you, for My strength is made perfect in weakness"* (2 Cor. 12:9).

In talking about the natural characteristics we have been given, we must not forget the supernatural: the power of God that comes into our lives at just the right time and enables us to do what we otherwise could not do. It has happened to me countless times. God to the rescue! He gives us strength in the midst of our weakness, and He alone gets the glory.

Many times, Karen would find herself in despair and not even wanting to go to whatever meeting we needed to attend. Then, in a time of ministry, God would show up. And whom did He show His mighty power through but the one who seemed to be weakest at the time! Karen would go from "stuck in the mud" to "soaring with the eagles"—speaking the words of God and bringing hope and encouragement to others when, just minutes before, she was struggling to move forward.

A few years ago, one of our missionaries asked me to come to India to speak. I had been there before and had enjoyed a wonderful time with the churches. On my first visit, I had spoken primarily to Christians and was asked to teach and encourage the thousand people who had gathered for the conference. This time, I was being asked to do an evangelistic campaign in a city where they had never held one. I told my missionary friend that I was happy to serve any way he would like me to, but that evangelism was not my strong point.

"I am mostly a teacher," I confessed.

"I think you are the one for the job," my friend encouraged.

So I went. As long as I live, I will never forget the second night of the conference. I could feel those eagle's wings lift me to share in a way that I knew was not just "me." I have a picture of myself looking at the 250 mostly Hindu people who came forward to accept Christ. In the picture, I am standing with my hands on my hips almost in disbelief as all those people stood before me. Wow!

Far too many times to count, God has empowered Karen and me to accomplish things that are just not in our natural character and God-given abilities. Sometimes He will even supernaturally help us to do things that are opposed to our nature. Remember "Jill," the hawk? I have watched her many times, influenced by the Holy Spirit, nurture and tenderly comfort the little woodland creatures that by nature she would gobble up. Remember "Jack"? I have watched him stand under the power of God and speak clear and life-changing messages to someone in need. I have seen him in his weakness rising up in Christ's strength.

I believe that God leaves our weakness in place to help us see Who we belong to and Whose power we depend on. As we become more dependent on His power and less dependent on our own, we become less defined by our hawk or turtle tendencies and become more like Christ. Christ was able to soar overhead and see the "big picture" when He needed to, but He also walked side by side with the people on the ground, touching them with His sensitivity and compassion.

As turtles grow more Christlike, more often than not, they grow wings. They learn to be content with God's specific call to walk through those valleys and take in all God intends for them to see. They sprout those wings as they learn to rely on the power of God to take them where it is impossible for them to go in their own strength or ability. They really can do *all things*...through *Christ*...who *strengthens* them. (See Philippians 4:13.)

As hawks grow more Christlike, as they learn to be less self-reliant and more God-reliant, they become more tender and compassionate. They become more sensitive as to when they need to stay quiet on the ground, slow down, and take the time to share the love of God with those He brings to them.

As we decrease and Christ increases in us, God will do amazing things that will astound us. We may even see turtles soar!

Chapter 4

Hawk-like!

Over our years of marriage, Karen and I have had some pretty heated discussions about our differences and that ever-looming question as to who is *right*—right about how to handle a given situation, about child-rearing, or about which sofa to buy. Of course, when we think about it in quieter times, when no "issue" is on the table, we can both confidently say that neither one of us is right; we are just different in our perspective and our ways. However, in the heat of battle, when for some unknown reason we are in conflict, being "right" seems really important—sometimes even a matter of life and death.

I believe that this attitude is fueled by an idea hidden deep in our hearts that has nothing to do with what we are wrong about, but rather that we ourselves are wrong: our nature and character, the way we look at things and approach life. Something inside rises up against appearing or being thought of that way! For some of us, it may touch painful wounds from childhood. We are wrong for even being here on this earth! For others of us, it is just pride we are defending. You don't have to be a rocket scientist to sense the inevitable conflicts this sort of thing would produce in the marriage of a turtle and a hawk. Discuss just about anything, and you can see the problems coming like a freight train. Yet, so often, God chooses two dramatically different personalities and says to them, "I have called you two to become one flesh." I will speak for many of us at this time and say to God in my most reverent voice, *"It just doesn't seem fair!"*

In the previous chapter, I talked of self-pity and some other tendencies of the turtle. Thus it is only right that we take a good hard look at those of us who are more hawk-like. Karen has often said to me, "You are just as much a sinner as I am, but your sins are more socially acceptable." As much as I hate to admit it, she's right. (Just don't tell her I said that!)

By "socially acceptable," she means that the tendencies we hawks have are not only tolerated but often praised within society, even though they may be contrary to God's ways. Have you ever heard of a football team called the Turtles? How about a track team with a tortoise as a mascot, or a swim team called the Sea Turtles? Turtles just don't strike fear in the hearts of opponents like Lions, Bears, Eagles, or Wildcats do. In our society, we want strong, aggressive action motivated by powerful, **self-reliant** leader-types. We want winners who know who they are and where they are going. We want success and numbers and good old-fashioned, never say die, pulled up by our own bootstraps, **self-made** hawks.

Now God often used very strong people to accomplish His purposes. No one I know has ever accused the apostle Paul of being a wishy-washy person. However, in Philippians 3, when he lists his accomplishments and qualifications, he concludes that in reality those things are "rubbish" (or "dung" in the King James Version) compared to what he could have in Christ; those traits and abilities are good for nothing, except maybe some fertilizer for the new life and knowledge he could have in Jesus.

I once thought these things were valuable, but now I consider them worthless because of what Christ has done. Yes, everything else is worthless when compared with the infinite value of knowing Christ Jesus my Lord. For His sake I have discarded everything else, counting it all as garbage, so that I could gain Christ and become one with Him (Philippians 3:7-9 NLT).

Hawks, by their very nature, tend to be "self" people, yet anything that originates in the many "self" words we have in our English language must come to death on the cross, along with the rest of our flesh. When Paul wrote the letter to believers in Rome, he told them that anything that is from our flesh, or natural man, must give way to the Spirit of God. *"For I know that in me* (that is, in my flesh) *nothing good dwells"* (Rom. 7:18). Every hawk-like attitude and attribute must be submitted to the work of the cross and the direction of the Spirit, or it becomes another effort of man to accomplish the work of the Kingdom of God.

The most convicting sermon (meaning that it convicted me the most) I have ever preached was on **self-righteousness**. Jesus came down harder on this characteristic of mankind than on any other area. Let's be honest here: We hawks often drip with it. The original Greek word means to be **self-right**. In other words, the **rightness** about an issue comes from within ourselves—not from God. We mistakenly think—and I want all of you hawks out there to hear this—that if we are **accurate** about something, then we have the right to defend our position to the death. What is worse is that we also think that God is behind us on it. Rightness from within is nothing more than the smelliest of all sins: self-righteousness. It is, however, one of the most socially acceptable of all sins. That should tell us something right there.

I will never forget the personal illustration that the Lord so lovingly gave to help me understand this. I love softball. I actually accepted Christ as my Savior on a Christian men's softball team. I am also very competitive and enjoy winning. (What can I say? I am a hawk!) I love the famous quote from legendary Green Bay Packers coach Vince Lombardi, "Winning isn't everything, it's the only thing." At any rate, the very weekend I was preparing my sermon on self-righteousness, the Lord stuck a mirror in front of my face and said to me, "Before you preach about that, take a good look at what it is." The game was on Friday night and the sermon on self-righteousness on Sunday. I won't bore you with all the details, but a situation came up where the umpire made a call that I was absolutely, 100-percent sure he was wrong about. I was on third base, and the call took a run away from us as the inning ended. In the heat of battle (and before I remembered I was the pastor of the church), I found myself challenging the ump on the call. Some choice phrases from my days before Christ came to mind: "Hey, ump, you want to borrow my glasses? You're missing a great game."

I once talked to one of the key leaders in the Athletes in Action organization. He told me that one of the best things about competition is that it quickly brings to the surface the sin in our hearts. Boy, have I found that to be true! I have since toyed with the idea of making one of the requirements for a position on the church board a full-court basketball game with the men in the congregation. We will quickly see what is in their hearts!

Now, back to the softball game. There is a procedure for challenging a call that an ump makes. It must be done by the team coach, which I was not. Fortunately, I bit my tongue before I made a fool out of myself and disgraced the Lord. I did go back to the dugout and discuss with my teammates the inaccuracy of the call. (Shame on me!)

I was sure I was right, but in essence I was all wrong— wrong because I was on that field to glorify the Lord Jesus Christ and be a witness to those who watched. I was there to show the guys on the team that you can be a Christian, love the Lord, play with all your might, and be a real man for Jesus. I was there to model to the church how to behave under pressure and walk with integrity. But, at that moment, I was doing none of those things. In my mind, my "accuracy" on the issue gave me the right to stand my ground and challenge the authority (the umpire). I was not defending the Lord's righteousness (which, by the way, doesn't need defending); I was championing my own **self-rightness**. It had come from *my* heart and mind, not from the spirit of God. *He* was not asking me to take a stand against injustice; it was all "ME."

It doesn't really matter whether or not we are accurate about a given situation. It is our response and the heart behind it that counts. Are we being obedient to the Holy Spirit or just voicing our own opinion? The Pharisees were accurate about the law concerning the woman caught in adultery, but they were wrong about what God's intention for her was at that moment. They were accurate about the laws concerning the

Sabbath, but wrong as to the Lord's compassionate desire to heal the poor souls who were suffering.

We can be accurate about how money is spent, how our children are disciplined, how a neighbor is treated, or about buying a dining room table, but totally miss what the Lord may have in mind for the money, our kids, the neighbor, or what's for dinner! God is intimately involved in our lives, and what He has in mind is what is *right*—and that's not necessarily the same as what we believe to be accurate. The Pharisees thought they were defending the ways of God, but as the Bible so often says, Jesus discerned their thoughts. In other words, He saw through the impure motives of their hearts and their self-rightness.

There is a way that seems right to a man, but its end is the way of death (Proverbs 14:12).

In perhaps the most famous of all of Jesus' teachings, the Sermon on the Mount, these immortal and powerful words were uttered: *"Blessed are the meek, for they shall inherit the earth"* (Matt. 5:5). Now many different words might be used to describe a hawk, but I sincerely doubt that "**meek**" would be one of them. When we hear the word *meek*, we automatically think of "weak"; mousy, spineless, gutless, and fearful come to mind. Yet, Jesus was the meekest of all and certainly none of those other things.

The meaning of this word has drifted far from what it was in the language of Jesus' day. In Greek, *meek* meant **strength under control**—a power and authority that would be used only under the direction of the master. I have heard that it was used to describe the most powerful Greek chariot horses: the ones that could carry the warriors into battle with speed and agility, yet were so well trained that they could be stopped, started, and turned on a dime at the slightest direction of the reins of the master. Life and death were at stake and depended on how yielded or how "meek" the horse was. Total surrender of our wills to His is what is required.

For most of us hawks, this lesson comes hard. By nature, we tend to be stubborn and self-willed and resist coming under the direction of others. Some use the excuse, "That's just the way the Lord made me," or "This is the way I am wired." Yet, unless that comes to death, we will not be fit for the Master's use. Just because something is natural to us does not mean it is right in God's eyes. In fact, the *natural* is often exactly opposite to the *spiritual*. Just because it's the way you are doesn't mean it is God's way.

Coming under the control of the Holy Spirit does not diminish our ability to be effective in the Kingdom of God. In fact, it is the only way to have any effect at all; it is where the real power comes from and the real work takes place. I will always remember the "meekest" horse I ever met; the picture of my interaction with this magnificent animal will forever be etched onto my heart. As a young man (not long after I had accepted the Lord), I began to work at a juvenile detention center near Phoenix, Arizona. I was put in charge of the animal program, which included chickens, goats, sheep, rabbits, a few cattle, and about 10-12 horses for the boys to ride. Occasionally, we would receive donations of some very fine horses to be used as a part of the rehabilitation process. The boys could earn the right to have their own horse by caring for them, and they also learned some valuable relationship skills through the process.

One day, we received a horse named Smokey. He was a beautiful, gray quarter horse that had just been retired as a polo pony. As horses go, he was not that old, but his owners had decided it was time to bring in a younger model and give Smokey some well-deserved rest. One look at him and even a novice like me could tell that this was a powerful animal. He had spent his life in training and competition and was in peak condition when he came to us. I have yet to see a more well-trained animal of any kind.

The day I went to pick him up at a nearby ranch, his owner opened the back door to my horse trailer and then Smokey's corral. To my amazement, Smokey walked out of the pen and straight into the trailer with only verbal commands from the owner. The first time I rode him, I knew that this was a special horse. The owner had instructed me that he was "rein-trained" and did not require a bit. (For us greenhorns, the bit is the piece of metal that goes in the horse's mouth to control it.) No such device was needed for Smokey. Simply lay the reins on the side of his neck, and he would turn on a dime. The first time I rode him, I almost ended up in a saguaro cactus a couple of times. I was going straight ahead, but I would accidentally brush the reins against one side of his neck or the other, and he would instantly make a sharp turn to that side. I could only imagine what he'd been like on the polo field, where directions must be obeyed immediately to be successful. Years of training had also strengthened his already powerful frame.

On one of our first rides, I had taken the boys with their horses out into the desert area around our ranch. The Central Arizona Project was digging a canal from the Colorado River to bring water to the metropolitan area of Phoenix. The huge waterway under construction had very steep banks that were maybe a hundred feet bottom to top. Many of the horses balked when we tried to ride them up the embankment, and for some it was even a bit of a struggle. As Smokey and I arrived, he kicked into high gear and powered his way to the top with unbelievable speed and strength, as I held on for dear life.

I have often thought of Smokey as a beautiful example of what the Lord's intentions are for those who serve Him. If we were that well-trained and the Lord could easily direct us without our kicking and bucking, what things could be accomplished for His Kingdom! For those of us who have the independent, self-reliant personality of the hawk, if we intend to be used by Him, we must learn to be guided by the smallest gestures of our Master. Psalm 32:8 really describes this desire of the Lord towards us: *"I will instruct you and teach you in the way you should go; I will guide you with My eye."* Wouldn't it be something if the Lord only had to glance in our direction to communicate His desires, and we would be quick to fulfill His plan? Verse 9 goes on to give the contrast: *"Do not be like the horse or like the mule, which have no understanding, which must be harnessed with bit and bridle, else they will not come near you"* (Ps. 32:9). I keep a bit right above my desk in my office to remind me of this critical spiritual principle. It is my choice as to how I will be guided.

Make no mistake about it. God will lead you, if you are His. It is your choice as to how. You can be guided by His eye and bring both pleasure and productivity to His Kingdom. Or you can choose the bit, which will bring some element of pain with it. It is out of His love for us that He guides us. He knows the "ways we should go." Smokey was no less of a horse by having yielded to such training. In fact, his value was increased many times because he responded so quickly. He was still powerful. He was still quick and agile. He was strong and dependable and a joy to ride. But he was *meek*: **strength under control!**

One final note: Remember the softball game where I challenged the umpire? When I got home that evening, I pulled out the rule book to settle the issue once and for all. Turns out I was wrong!

CHAPTER 5

And They Both Lived "Happily Ever After"

More than one-third of marriages that take place in the United States today end, sadly, in divorce. I can't help thinking of this as I stand before a couple on the joyous day of their marriage and pronounce them "husband and wife." Will they be a part of this statistic after a few turmoil-filled years of marriage? I do my best to prepare them for the "covenant" they are choosing to enter into, but currents in the river of our modern society prove to be strong when it comes to divorce.

There are strong pulls on all of us to think of our vows more from a worldly point of view. Since the beginning of man's history on this earth, there has been a struggle for us between doing things *God's way* or *our way*. Adam and Eve were the first of many who have bit the "apple" of things God has deemed off limits. Is God trying to deny us good things that will bring us pleasure? Absolutely not! Like the wise, loving Father that He is, He only desires what is best for us. Our "best" comes when we fully obey His ways and put Him first in our lives. If anyone or anything else takes precedence, the Bible calls it "idolatry."

Many of us, when we hear the word "idolatry," we picture someone kneeling before some huge statue of an animal or deity and offering a sacrifice while natives chant in the background. Yet, in actuality, *an idol is anything that has become more important to us than what God has commanded or a higher priority in our lives than God Himself.*

We can make an idol of money. Even though we do not bow down and worship it, the pursuit of money can often take God's rightful place as our top priority. How many times have I heard someone say they would come to church, but they're so tired from their week's work that they must rest on Sunday? Most of these people have all the basics of life, but they want more and put that ahead of God.

Things can become idols. Cars, houses, pets, all sorts of material stuff can take the part of our heart that belongs to God. Recreation has certainly become an idol in this country. We pursue leisure activity with passion, spending millions of dollars a year. Why? Because we have worked so hard earning more money that we need more time and ways to relax. Meanwhile, obedience and honoring God move farther down the list of priorities in our lives.

God was not kidding when He gave Moses the Ten Commandments beginning with *"Thou shalt have no other gods before Me."* Those were not the "ten suggestions"; they were the "ten commandments" given to help us keep our lives in proper order. God is not egotistical, but He demands our undivided attention. Life will not work very well for us if He doesn't have it! A very high percentage of our marriage problems could be solved if we would always put God and His ways as our top priority.

Over the past several decades, an idolatrous belief has crept into the hearts and minds of even those in the church. This belief is that we have every right to, and even deserve, a happy marriage and life. *Happiness* can also become an idol in our lives. How many couples have stood before a judge and said these words, "I am just not happy"? I have heard them countless times in my office or over a cup of coffee with those whom I counsel. "Doesn't God want us to be happy?"

Happiness is sometimes a by-product of obedience and righteousness (doing what is right according to God), *but not always!* Happiness is usually connected to circumstance, so it comes and goes. It is tied to the word "happening." And although happiness has become the goal of many marriages, it should not be. We have adopted a worldly view that if we are not happy, we have the right to make changes in our lives that *will* make us happy. "Happiness" is usually based in our self-centered desire for comfort and getting our needs met. Just look at the advertisements we are bombarded with daily from every angle: "You deserve the best"; "You're worth it"; "You deserve a break today." From hair color to fast food, from the car we drive to our retirement, the message is loud and clear: "You deserve to be happy at all costs."

Unfortunately, those costs have become our marriages and often our children. This message has most certainly affected our relationship with God. The goal of our marriages *should* be to be *right* with God—in right standing with Him, living a life of obedience to what the Bible tells us are His ways. That often results in happiness, *but not always!*

What does that really mean? Let me see if I can illustrate.

I have been preaching on one of the greatest and most impacting of Jesus' many discourses, the "Sermon on the Mount." Jesus delivered it near the beginning of His ministry, and it contains some earth-shattering statements. His discourse begins with the nine *"beatitudes"* (Latin for "blessing"), which all start with the words: "Blessed are...." Some newer translations use the word "happy" in place of "blessed." I asked a friend of mine, who is a Greek and Hebrew scholar, if this was an accurate translation. He told me that happiness is included in the meaning of the word "blessed" in both languages but is far too simple a definition to fully describe the word. He went on to say that the most accurate translation would be "to be spoken well of by God." That has a far different meaning than "happy."

Sometimes, as Christians, we are happy when we are obeying God's Word (and sometimes we are not), but *we are always spoken well of by God when we obey Him.* Here is an example from my own life. On one of my trips to India, my two teammates and I got hold of some really bad chicken meat. We were usually served wonderful meals while working there, but on this occasion all three of the team became deathly ill. Our puny American stomachs could not handle whatever was in that chicken. There is no refrigeration in the area, and everything is "fresh," so to speak.

We were staying in a house that was about 400 yards from the main complex where we were to be the key speakers. It was the first evening of a four-day conference. As the three of us made our way down the dirt road to the complex, we had to stop about every 50 feet to catch our breath and try not to throw up. I don't know when I have ever been so sick. We were as white as sheets, and all of us wondered how we were going to stand in the heat for the next three hours and teach and preach to the nearly 1,200 eager participants.

Kevin, one of our trio, happened to pull a flyer out of his Bible at one of our "rest stops." He made kind of a sick chuckle and handed it to me. There on the flyer were our names, accompanied by the purpose of the evening meetings: "Reverend Carl Hampsch, Reverend Kevin Neely and Peter Gilmartin...Healing and Miracle Crusade." Here we were, all sicker than dogs and, ironically, the main speakers and prayer warriors at a healing meeting.

By God's grace and mercy, we made it through the night without fainting or "tossing our cookies." Kevin wobbled a little once but he caught himself before keeling over. As usual, God's strength was shown in our weakness, and there were many saved and many healed that night. Unfortunately, not us! Now, let me tell you, we were not *happy* that night, but were we ever *blessed*! I believe that God "spoke well" of our little team of weaklings, but we were not happy...

The last of the beatitudes is, *"Blessed are those who are persecuted for righteousness' sake, for theirs is the kingdom of heaven"* (Matt. 5:10). The many saints before us, as well as those today, who suffer incredible persecution for their faith are probably often not happy. Many have given their lives in horrible situations, for the cause of Christ. I cannot imagine that anyone could be happy while being burned at the stake. They are, however, spoken well of by God. Why? Because they are standing for what is right and obeying Jesus' commands.

Our number one priority in life should be to be "blessed" (spoken well of) by God. Can you imagine anything more important in life? We are "blessed" by God when we fully obey His direction for us in life and in marriage. Think back to what I tell young couples during my premarital sessions with them: "The primary purpose and highest calling of marriage is that together you can be more effective for God's Kingdom than you could as singles." It is why we were created and why God brings us a life-partner: for His purposes. It is not necessarily just to be happy. It is all about Him, not us. We are sometimes happy in marriage and sometimes not. The important thing is that we are doing what is right in God's eyes, not making happiness another idol that takes the place reserved for Him.

I have sat in on my share of marriage-oriented ministry seminars and teachings over the years. Many seem to have an underlying motive of happiness as a goal in marriage. Communication is important and helpful in marriage; so is problem-solving and a healthy sexual relationship; but if the sole purpose of attending these is a happy marriage, my experience is that relief from conflict may come, but it is usually temporary.

The idol of happiness has become a major foundation of our society and is woven into our lives even as children. Think about our fairy tales: The ultimate goal of Prince Charming and the Fair Maiden is to live "happily ever after." If they are not happy, many a Fair Maiden believes she must have the wrong Prince Charming and begins looking for another. And how many times does the Prince want to put his Sleeping Beauty back to sleep because she is not making him happy? Their goal *should* be to live "*blessed* ever after," which is what happens when they fully obey the Lord.

For Karen and me, repentance from worshiping our idol of happiness has been a key to a committed and blessed relationship. To "repent" means to sigh deeply in grief for our sin and to stop doing what you are doing and go the other direction. Now we put being in right standing with God above being happy. When you get things in the order God intended, it is amazing how much better life will go for you.

Getting in "right standing with God" means looking at your life and asking Him what is out of order, using the Bible and God's commandments as your guide. Although Karen and I are still in the process of doing this, we have both found that the deep *joy* of obeying Christ is far more satisfying than the uncertainty of "happiness." Jesus said that if anyone wanted to follow Him, they would need to deny themselves and take up their cross every day. That does not sound like a happy experience, and this "dying to self" stuff has not been fun. However, for me it has produced the fruit of joy that comes only from being right in God's eyes and obeying Him. It is a rich blessing, right to the core of your being.

I would never trade joy for happiness. I appreciate both of them, but to me *happiness* is like whipped cream and *joy* like a big, juicy T-bone steak! They are both tasty food items, but one brings a much greater inner strength and long-lasting energy to endure life's challenges. I like whipped cream; however, I do not need it to sustain my life. Protein (or joy) is something I cannot live without.

I am asking you to re-think the foundation of your marriage relationship. Let's be honest here. How many of us, when we first saw our mate-to-be, thought to ourselves, "Wow, now there is a girl/guy who would make me more effective for God's

Kingdom"? Most of us were probably thinking (either consciously or unconsciously), "Now there is someone who could really meet my needs," whether that be physical, emotional, or even spiritual. In our carnal minds, we generally think about our needs first.

God is aware of our needs. In Genesis 2:18 (NIV), God said of Adam, *"It is not good for the man to be alone. I will make a helper suitable for him."* That word *"helper"* means a completer or someone to make us whole. For what purpose though? So we will be "happy"? Or so we will be a more complete and balanced being for His service?

God has blessed Karen and me with so many things that bring great pleasure to our marriage relationship. He meant them to be a blessing and joy to us, not for us to make them idols and worship them ahead of Him. Paul spoke of idolatry in Romans 1:25, "[They] *exchanged the truth of God for the lie, and worshiped and served the creature rather than the Creator, who is blessed forever. Amen."*

Jesus told us that we are here to *serve*, not to *be served*. I believe that we will find true contentment, joy, and fulfillment in our lives, and marriages, when we are being what God created us to be. We were created to serve and worship Him, not to serve ourselves and idols such as *happiness*. We are here for God's good pleasure!

CHAPTER 6

Idols in Marriage: Those Who Make Them Will Be Like Them

We are each accountable to the Lord for how we respond to the things that come into our lives, many of which are unfair, unjust, undeserved, and even cruel. God wants us to respond in forgiveness, not bitterness. However, we may have trouble forgiving those who have hurt us because doing that seems like we are letting them off the hook, even saying that what they did was acceptable. That is not what forgiveness does; it doesn't simply let offenders off the hook. Moreover, practicing forgiveness doesn't mean that we should continue to let others be hurtful to us without establishing boundaries. Rather, *forgiving others means trusting God to take care of (or deal with) those who have offended us.* They are accountable to Him, and He is always just.

When we hold on to past hurts and offenses, we are just loading ourselves down with things God didn't intend for us to carry. Jesus said it this way in Matthew 11:30: *"My yoke is easy and My burden is light."* Here is another illustration from our marriage that I hope will shed further light on this process. It has to do with the very interesting verses in Psalm 115 that are in the title of this chapter.

Most of us come into marriage with "baggage," which is a polite way of saying that we are burdened by sinful responses to life's pain, our sinful ways of coping with life, rather than turning to God. Karen and I brought our own matching set into our marriage. Our first 15 years were filled with some wonderful joys—and some difficult challenges. Some of those resulted in a dark (and very deep) time of depression for Karen, and it brought a coming-to-death to some of my "self"-ways.

Besides the incredible weight of the depression, guilt was overwhelming Karen. She had known the Lord for over 30 years with a great knowledge of the Word. Why wasn't the Holy Spirit able to overcome this depression in her? Was there something so wrong with her that God would not help? All of this took a huge toll on her confidence as a Christian and in her relationships, including our marriage. Also satan, the enemy of our souls, was quick to add his dose of condemnation and accusation to the mix, which certainly intensified things.

Meanwhile, God was working deeply in my life as well, pointing out my baggage and asking me to get rid of it. Mine was more "socially acceptable" perhaps, but it was still sin. It had to do with my self-reliance, wrong motives, and pride, which kept me from needing God. Here is how God revealed our idolatry:

Karen and I had gone to a wonderful ministry called *Elijah House* in North Idaho (which has since moved to Spokane, Washington) for marriage counseling. The Lord ended up moving us to the area where we now pastor our church. We received prayer ministry there on a somewhat regular basis, and God began unloading the weight of our sin, one thing at a time. It had been a long haul, and both of us were pretty worn out. Although much progress was made, we were not out of the woods yet. One day, we were together at a session, and Karen shared some very difficult, heart-wrenching issues with the prayer minister. There were many tears and hurts—it was intense! Karen excused herself to go to the restroom. The prayer minister looked squarely at me and asked, "How are you doing with all this?"

Although God has given me an extra measure of stamina (which sometimes works against me as God is wearing me down), I was near exhaustion. I replied, "I feel like Karen has been hanging over the edge of a cliff for years now, and I don't know how much longer I can hold on to her."

She responded with this short but life-changing statement: "Why don't you let her go?"

I thought, *That's out of the question. How could I do that? She is my wife! How could a person of the Lord ask such a thing?* Yet, I could not get the idea out of my head. The Holy Spirit had just dropped a bomb on me.

By God's design, Karen and I had taken separate cars to the appointment, so it was just me and God in the car afterward. As I drove away, in my mind there was this huge neon sign blinking those words: "Let her go… Let her go… Let her go." It went against something deeply imbedded in me, and I wrestled with it for several miles. But God won (as He always does), for which I am eternally grateful.

I could show you the exact spot on the freeway where I surrendered. (I should ask the highway department to let me put up one of those historical markers there, as that moment changed the course of our lives.) I prayed this simple prayer, which I think is one of my greatest prayers ever: "Lord, I give up!"

Suddenly, a vivid picture flashed into my mind. Karen was hanging over the edge of the cliff, which I instinctively knew was life-threatening although I couldn't see what lay below. She had a large rope tied around her waist. I was holding the rope, in a grip of desperation, seated with my feet dug in, much like someone in a tug-of-war with a formidable opponent. I could see the skid marks in the dirt that my heels had made. I was obviously losing ground. My face was red with exhaustion, and sweat poured off me.

That picture expressed my feelings exactly. The years of struggle had literally brought me to the end of my strength (and my rope). I knew that I could hold on no longer. I said out loud, "Okay, Lord, I am letting go of Karen!"

I saw myself releasing the rope. The picture suddenly zoomed back so I could see the scene from a greater distance. To my amazement, the rope that was tied to Karen moved only an inch or two and stopped. I could see clearly that it went through my hands, under my arms, and extended behind me another 15 feet or so where it was tied to the most massive oak tree one could imagine. Boy, did I feel foolish! For all these years, I thought *I* had been holding Karen and had expended a lot of energy doing so. Now I could see that I never had her in the first place—it was God all along. He alone is faithful and able to keep us in every way. He alone is our Savior and our help in trouble. He alone can hold us from falling and destruction. And He alone deserves the glory, for He is God!

Let me share with you the lessons we have learned from this. First, I should tell you, this happened about ten years ago, and we have never been the same. What does this have to do with idolatry, you might ask? Well, from Karen's view, when she looked back at what was holding her from falling, she would naturally see me. From her perspective, I was her only chance for survival. No wonder she was depressed! She had been looking to me to be her savior and to rescue and fix her, and I had tried hard to do just that. But I was out of order. That was God's job and His alone.

Karen had made me an idol, and I had gladly stepped up on the platform to take my place. Why? Because I like to be looked at as a savior. It feels good, for a while anyway, to be depended upon by someone, to be their fixer and rescuer. That was sin in my heart! I wanted to be God to Karen. Impure motives had kept me in this place until, by God's grace, I had become too exhausted. For Karen, the answer was to repent for putting me in the place that only Jesus can occupy. He paid for her sins, and He has earned the place of Savior in her life. He has the power to forgive her sins, heal her heart, and set her free. *Jesus* is her Savior, King, Healer, and Rescuer—not me.

Several major things happened in our marriage. Almost immediately, I felt the release from not holding onto Karen. What a relief! Repentance is so sweet; it gets us in right order with God and takes away the loads we were not meant to carry. Second, it greatly encouraged Karen. Now, when she looks at who is holding her, she sees the incredible strength of the Almighty represented in the mighty oak. She can relax, as well, knowing she is safe in His care.

My role now is pointing to the Lord as Karen looks at me. The power of the Lord pulled Karen onto solid ground, and I can encourage her to depend on Him. I believe this is the right order in God. We have a very definite role as husband and wife to point each other to Jesus. It is the most loving thing we can do. All of us have days when we're hanging over the edge and feel like we are about to lose it, never to return. Jesus is always the answer!

God spoke to Karen in a very unique way as well. The more she looked to me to hear the cry of her heart, the less I seemed to be able to help her. She was desperate for me to save her, but I could not. One day, at the point of total frustration, she called out to God, and the words she used shocked even her. "You are doing this to me, aren't You, God?"

She suddenly realized that the more she looked to me to save her, the less God would let me respond. That is when the Lord led her to the verses in Psalm 115. She and I had made an idol of our marriage. The beginning verses of that chapter go like this.

> *Not unto us, O Lord, not unto us, but to Your name give glory.... Our God is in heaven; He does whatever He pleases. Their idols are silver and gold, the work of men's hands. They have mouths, but they do not speak; eyes they have, but they do not see; they have ears, but they do not hear; noses they have, but they do not smell; they have hands, but they do not handle; feet they have, but they do not walk; nor do they mutter through their throat. Those who make them are like them; so is everyone who trusts in them* (Psalm 115:1,3-8).

For Karen, this is exactly what had happened. I became just what this verse illustrates. I have a mouth but could not speak to the need in Karen's life. I have eyes but could not see how to fix her. I have ears but could not hear the cry of her heart or know what to do about it if I could. This is God's love and mercy toward us. Otherwise, we live serving idols and not Him. We would never realize the great joy and freedom He has for us, and we would just settle for the temporary and incomplete salvation our spouse would bring.

I know that there are many of you out there who can relate to this story. You may be the one who is hanging over the cliff. Let me strongly advise you to not look to your spouse to be your savior. They cannot save you; and because God loves you, He will not let them. Remember the first commandment, *"You shall have no other gods before Me!"* He really means that. All other gods will mess things up. Just ask Karen. Furthermore, if you are the one holding the rope, I strongly advise you to let it go! Take it from me, you were never intended to bear that load. If need be, God will let you wear yourself out until you have to let go. Pray the greatest prayer for yourself: "Lord, I give up!"

Others may identify with the picture of idols who cannot speak, hear, or see. You may feel like you speak Russian while your spouse speaks Chinese. No matter how hard you try, they are not able to hear you or see your heart. Maybe the "Lord is doing it" or, at least, allowing it. You may have some repenting to do for making an idol of your marriage or spouse. You may be looking to them to meet the needs that only God can (and *wants* to) meet.

Recently, I had the joy of doing a number of weddings. I love the "traditional" marriage service, even though I am not a very traditional person. A particular line stood out to me as I read this last Saturday:

The union of husband and wife in heart, body, and mind is intended by God for their mutual joy [Note: "joy" not "happiness"], for the help and comfort given to one another in prosperity and adversity, and when it is God's will, for the procreation of children and their nurture in the knowledge and love of the Lord. Therefore, marriage is not to be entered into unadvisedly or lightly, but soberly, deliberately, and in the reverent fear before God. Into this holy union, these two have now come to be joined.

What a powerful statement about God's plan for marriage! We should "help and comfort" (*not* "save and fix") in the "reverent fear before God." *Fear* is respect for who He is and who we are not.

If you are ready to get things in order, grab your husband or wife (as the case may be), and get down on your knees together. Apologize to each other and repent for being out of order with God. Ask forgiveness of each other, whether you have been the one over the edge with the rope tied to you or the one holding on. Then ask God to forgive you for the idolatry you have created in your marriage, and for looking someplace other than Him for your salvation, or for putting yourself in His place. The Bible tells us that He is faithful and just to forgive us our sins, *if* we confess them to Him and to those we have sinned against.

Some of you may need to repent for making happiness more important than being right with God. When you get things in His order, you will be amazed at how life goes so much better. It is the way He created us to live. *"Apart from Him we can do nothing!"* (See John 15:5 NLT.)

CHAPTER 7

Turtle and Hawk Crossing Ahead!

M ost of us, at one time or another, have seen the road signs that have a picture of an antlered deer in mid-stride with a *"Warning! Deer Crossing ahead"* notice. One year, while bow-hunting in northern Arizona, I observed something interesting about them. Some friends and I had a tradition of hunting together for a week near the north rim of the Grand Canyon, which is famous for "big bucks." We were several days into our hunt and had hardly seen a deer. We had checked our favorite water holes and meadows, and it seemed as though all the deer had received a notice of the season's start and had vacated the area. We found ourselves driving farther and farther from camp to try to find them.

On one particular stretch of road, we happened to see two deer cross at approximately the same place. Since they were about the only living things we had seen for days, we decided to investigate. Next morning, we drove that road at about the same time. Lo and behold, we spotted yet another deer cross the highway at almost the same spot. We pulled our truck off the blacktop where the buck had disappeared into the forest. One of the more observant members of our group pointed at the bright yellow sign directly in front of the truck: *"Warning— Deer Crossing."*

No way! We had always assumed that those signs were just randomly placed in deer country to warn drivers of the possibility of collision with unsuspecting animals. More investigation of the area, however, revealed a very well-worn game trail that led right to the spot where the sign was placed. It continued on the other side of the highway. Being the incredible trackers (and students of wildlife) that we were, we spent the rest of the week hunting in the area.

The very day that we made our brilliant discovery, I began building a tree-stand above the trail, about a quarter-mile off the highway. There I was, 25 feet up in an aspen tree hammering away on the stand, when some movement caught my eye. There, standing on the trail near the base of the tree, was a beautiful buck and doe staring up at me. On the ground several feet away from the inquisitive deer...lay my expensive bow and arrows. *That figures!*

Although none of us filled our tags that year, we saw deer every day. Game trails are well-traveled animal "freeways"; even a novice hunter knows that they are a good place to hunt. They connect the feeding, watering, and safe bedding areas. They are pathways to the essentials of life.

Jesus made a trail for us to follow that would lead us to the essentials of life. In fact, He told His disciples that if any of them wanted to follow Him, they would need to use this trail, and only this trail. He said in Mark 8:34 (NIV): *"If anyone would come after Me, he must deny himself and take up his cross and follow Me."* This incredible statement must have turned the heads of everyone within earshot. "What did He just say? We must not have heard that correctly. Did He say 'take up your cross'?"

There was most likely not one among them who had not witnessed the gruesome torture that the Romans used to keep the masses in line with only relatively small numbers of soldiers. Most of them had heard the pleading of those who hung for days, slowly suffocating to death. They dared not help the crucified ones, lest they take their place on the cross. Mankind had seldom slumped so low in history. Such a slow and painful death could not be what He meant. After all, things were going so well. The crowds had just recently rejoiced as a blind man had been healed in Bethesda. They had marveled at the miracle of the feeding of the 4,000 with seven small loaves of bread. And Peter had just proclaimed Jesus to be the Christ, the Messiah, and the One they had all been waiting for. What is all this talk about a cross? What does that have to do with following the Messiah? How could this instrument of torture be a part of discipleship? Understanding what Jesus was saying in these commands about the cross would be a lifelong endeavor for them, for us, and for all mankind. One thing is certain—it is the trail that Jesus has not only gone on before us, but directed all disciples to follow.

Dying to our self! What a tall order. It goes against everything in our culture. We are inundated with media that encourages us to do just the opposite: Pamper yourself, spoil yourself, protect yourself, and above all else do not die to self! Yet this command and challenge from Christ is just as poignant today as it was the day He spoke it. It is especially critical in marriage because that's the place where our two selves bump into each other most.

Galatians chapter 5 talks about this epic battle between our flesh and our spirit. Paul tells us in verse 17 that the two are *"contrary to one another"* or "opposite" of each other. How true! With Karen and I, when we are in a conflict where we are contrary to each other, it is most often my flesh that is in conflict with hers.

If I were going to try to list the conflicts that this "flesh versus flesh" has caused in our marriage, a single book would not be enough; I would need *volumes!* It happens often. For example, I come home from a long and stressful day at the office. (Maybe some of you have heard these statistics: Men use about 5,000 words per day, while women use about 20,000. Admittedly, this scientific research is inconclusive, and sometimes even has the opposite findings—according to *Psychology Today* and many others—yet with Karen and I it seems roughly accurate.) I have had one meeting after another and have spoken twice the number of words most males use on the average. Karen, on the other hand, has been running kids around and doing housework and is about 10,000 words short.

So, while I am all talked out, she is excited to see me and get all caught up with the meaningful conversations of the day. In detail! Meanwhile I notice on the clock that the baseball game I have been waiting for all week has already started. My flesh is tired and wants to veg out. Her flesh is getting offended that I am not paying attention to her needs.

Now both of us have legitimate claims. I need some silence and time to unwind. Karen needs some quality relationship time with me. Our flesh does need care and feeding. However, it is often at this point that someone's flesh begins complaining. If we are not really careful, a conflict is at hand. To add to the problem, our flesh tends to store up ammunition for future conflicts:

"This is the third time this week you have come home too tired to talk to me," she might say.

"Well, I came home yesterday and talked for hours even though I was exhausted," I shoot back. Like the Hatfields and McCoys, we fire away until we are out of ammo or get mortally wounded.

I have heard it said that our flesh is really not, in and of itself, evil; it just wants to serve God on its own terms. Our flesh is a part of who God created us to be. It has needs and wants and is a critical part of who we are. It is important and necessary. It houses our soul and spirit. The key is that our flesh must be under the control of the Holy Spirit. If it is not, it can easily participate in those awful deeds that Paul lists for us in Galatians 5:19-21—things like *"jealousies, outbursts of wrath, selfish ambitions,"* and much worse.

I have seen these things come out of me in my battles with Karen. It is not pretty. Our flesh must remain in submission to the Spirit. Walking or living in the Spirit helps us to not fulfill the lust or demands of the flesh. Verse 24 of this same chapter sums it up: *"And those who are Christ's have crucified the flesh with its passions and desires"* (Gal. 5:24). Here is that process that Jesus spoke of and the trail He made for us. It sure is not easy, even sounds morbid. Crucify ourselves! Yet, it brings wonderful life to us in ways we never imagined.

This process is twofold. We must die if we want the resurrection life. For many of us the term "resurrection life" is a very religious sounding concept that we do not relate to. Because we do not have a clear picture of what lies ahead, we often have difficulty letting go of the life we are living. This new life we are promised is full of freedom. It is a life that will bring us the deep joy and satisfaction that we all are seeking. The only problem is that we can't have old life and new life both at the same time. We must be willing to let go of a life dictated by the flesh.

I once read a short story on how to catch a monkey. Apparently this really works! Jungle folk have learned to place clay jars with a small opening just big enough for a monkey's hand in areas frequented by the little creatures. In the jar they place favorite monkey snacks and tie the jar down to a stake. The monkeys find the jars and reach in and grab the snack in their hands. Now, with snack in hand, they can no longer remove their fist through the small opening. Something in them refuses to let go of the things inside the jar even though it will mean being easily caught.

I find myself doing the same thing. I grab hold of things that appeal to the fleshly part of me and refuse to let go, even if it means I will become captive to those things. Can you relate to that? It can be things like unforgiveness and resentment towards others; it can be an identity we have adopted. It can be rights that we believe we deserve, and as silly as it sounds, it can be represented in things like how we squeeze the toothpaste tube. It is anything in our flesh that we get that grip on and refuse to let go of. We become its slave.

Resurrection life comes from letting go of our ways and trusting that God has a better plan. He does! Romans 12:2 says it this way: *"Do not be conformed to this world, but be transformed...."* The Greek word for "conformed" means to be molded by something. It is like taking a piece of clay and shaping it around an object. It takes on the exact shape of that object. In this case, it is the world's ways.

"Transformed," on the other hand, is a total change in appearance and even in basic nature. The Greek word here is *metamorphoo*, and it is where we get the English word "metamorphosis." This is the wondrous process of the caterpillar turning into a beautiful butterfly. That is what God wants to do in our lives. He takes us as we are—turtles, hawks, and caterpillars—and through death to our ways and that wondrous "resurrection process," He makes us new creatures. We must be willing to "let go" of those things that are holding us captive in order for "transformation" to take place. If we are going to be resurrected with Christ, we must first be willing to die with Him.

Does that mean that we are all supposed to join monasteries and give up all fleshly comforts? Well, God may call some to that, but for most of us that is probably not His plan. It means changing bosses in our lives. Where the flesh has been CEO of our lives, it is time for a demotion. We are not going to fire him or her, just move them to a lesser position. The Holy Spirit must be our guide and rule. Christ becomes the influencer in our lives and in our decisions, no matter how small or great. When this happens, transformation occurs. We begin to become more Christlike.

In our marriage, when we are living ruled by the Spirit, we become more sensitive and attentive to the needs of each other. I am more in tune with when Karen really needs quality time with me. She becomes more aware of when I need to unwind and let the dust settle a bit. Do we do it right all the time? I wish! So does Karen. We are making progress though and becoming more Christlike, even in our marriage.

In recent years, the "WWJD" (What Would Jesus Do) slogan has become very popular. It reminds us that we are to be followers in the actions and attitude of Christ, then praise the Lord! What would Jesus do? He would yield to the desire and the plan of His Father and lay aside His thoughts and ways. If we are going to wear it, we must live it!

So what does it look like for a hawk and turtle to be willing to let go of their ways and live the surrendered life in Christ? To me it means being willing at any moment to give way to God's plan in our lives. For the hawk, it means being willing to walk for a while with your beloved. It means being patient (a fruit of the Spirit, by the way) when everything in you wants to soar. You will not always be ground-bound, of course—God made you a hawk for a reason—just when the heart of God desires it of you. For the turtle, it might mean taking more risks and doing a bit of flying from time to time. It might mean resisting the temptation of pulling back into the shell when danger is present or your hawk is in a mood.

Never underestimate the transforming power of Jesus! In frustration we can sometimes become hopeless, doubting that either our beloved spouse or we ourselves will ever become transformed. It is a difficult road for many of us, I will grant you that, but the Lord has made a promise to us to complete the job He started: of transforming our lives. How easy or how hard that goes depends on us.

I came across a beautiful passage of Scripture that reinforces this wonderful work of Christ in us. It is Isaiah 11:6-9:

> *The wolf also shall dwell with the lamb, the leopard shall lie down with the young goat, the calf and the young lion and the fatling together; and a little child shall lead them. The*

*cow and the bear shall graze; their young ones shall lie down
together; and the lion shall eat straw like the ox. The nurs-
ing child shall play by the cobra's hole, and the weaned child
shall put his hand in the viper's den. They shall not hurt nor
destroy in all My holy mountain, **for the earth shall be
full of the knowledge of the Lord** as the waters cover the
sea.*

What an amazing passage! The first part of Isaiah 11 speaks
of the coming of Jesus Christ to a fallen world. This is the result
and the effect that He can have on the very nature of creation:
The natural tendencies of even enemies are transformed to har-
mony and peace. *The wolf can dwell with the lamb!* Not just tolerate each other but dwell together.

I believe that the key for this transformation is given at the
end of the passage. *"For the earth shall be full of the knowledge of
the Lord...."* It is the knowledge of God's ways in our lives and
knowledge of who He is. It is the knowledge of His desire to
make us a new creature and our cooperation with that transforming work. It is the knowledge that He has chosen a coun-
terpart for us in marriage who may have natural ways very
opposite from ours; and the knowledge that in transformation,
God gets the glory.

You see, no one is amazed when two wolves dwell together
in unity. But a wolf and a lamb together—now that is a miracle! A leopard and a young goat—hallelujah, God is good! A
turtle and a hawk... WOW, He really is the Son of God! So, no
longer do we have just a hawk and a turtle, but rather a
Christian hawk and a Christian turtle. To be *"Christian"* means
that we are to be Christlike. When we follow Jesus on the trail
He cut for us by way of the cross and into the new life He has

made available to us, we become transformed. When people look at us, they may see the turtle or hawk, but mostly they begin to see Jesus reflected in our eyes.

John the Baptist said it best, "I must decrease, and He must increase." This is the natural way of the disciple of Christ. It becomes less and less important who we are and what we are all about. Jesus becomes everything! We no longer care what our strengths and weaknesses are. We just want with all of our hearts to be more like Him. Remember the words of that old hymn:

Turn your eyes upon Jesus,
Look full in His wonderful face,
And the things of earth will grow strangely dim
In the light of His glory and grace.

That is exactly what happens when we follow Him in this process. Being a hawk or a turtle is of very little importance. The light of His glory overshadows whatever we might (or might not) want others to see us as.

Jesus also said it this way in Mark 8:35: *"Whoever desires to save his life will lose it, but whoever loses his life for My sake and the gospel's will save it."* In other words, it means letting go of our old ways and old fleshly patterns. "Letting go" of the things that we are desperately hanging onto is, of course, the key to this transformation in our lives.

Maybe some of you have heard the story of the mountain climber who was nearing the top of the steep precipice he was climbing. Suddenly he lost his footing and, just as he fell, grabbed a branch. There he was, hanging hundreds of feet above the jagged rocks below. Unable to reach the rock wall, and with no other means of help, in desperation he called out, "Is anyone up there who can help me?" he cried.

A deep and majestic voice came thundering down from the top of the mountain. "I can," the voice replied.

"Who are you?" the desperate climber asked.

"It is Me, God," the deep voice responded.

"What do You want me to do?" the climber, now losing his grip, anxiously inquired.

"Let go!" was the unexpected answer from on high.

A long, thoughtful moment of silence followed, and then the man hanging from the branch asked, "Is there anyone *else* up there?"

It may not be easy to let go and let God take control, but it's worth it!

CHAPTER 8

Ways and Paths

God knows us all too well. And why wouldn't He? He created every cell in our bodies and every hair on our heads. Psalm 139 gives an in-depth understanding of this. Verse 3 says, *"You comprehend my path and my lying down, and are acquainted with all my ways."* God knows our paths, our natural ways of responding to life. Noah Webster's 1828 *American Dictionary of the English Language* describes a path as "a way beaten or trodden by the feet of man or beast." In other words, someone, or some animal, has used the same route so often that it becomes a path. Left to ourselves, we will go on the same track over and over again, even when it's not God's choice for us. We really are creatures of habit.

The word "way" is much the same. The dictionary mentioned above defines it as a "method or manner of practice." Growing up in a sinful world, we learn to cope with and survive life. A method of coping, a "way" used over and over again, becomes a "path." For example, as a child, if our "way" of coping with painful situations was to turn to God in our need and trust Him for comfort and healing, and it thus became a "path" in our lives, how wonderful! Unfortunately, most of us have not had that experience. Our fleshly "way" of dealing with life's pain is usually different. The "paths" we create are often not God's design for our lives.

It has been my experience that it usually takes significant pressure to force us off our paths. One of the things that God often uses to apply significant pressure is our marriage. In divorce situations, it is often that pressure that people are running from and not the "wicked spouse." The problem is that most of us do not even realize we are on a "fleshly path," and therefore we resist the pressure. Because of continuous use, these paths become part of our identity. To alter them would mean to change ourselves at the very core. But what the Lord wants is to change what we have become.

About a year or two after our marriage, Karen began expressing her concern for my inability to empathize with her when she was going through a difficult emotional time. "Where are you?" she would ask. "When I come to you hurting and in need, you seem to just disappear and become very distant." Karen is an emotional person, and this is the way God designed her. As the years have gone by, I have come not only to accept this but also to value it. As Karen puts it, she "feels things deeply."

Jesus was not ruled by His emotions, but He was often "moved with compassion" to intervene on behalf of those in need. Karen has accused me of being shallow and, indeed, sometimes I am. I would much rather skip across the shallows and not drift down into the depths, where often despair and gloom await. Karen began to realize there was something more to my response (or lack of it) than just a personality difference.

But I resisted! I would tell her, "You are too emotional. I am fine; it's you who has the problem." Sound familiar to any of you? Among my many flaws is a stubborn streak. Someone once told me that stubbornness is misdirected faith. (I am holding onto that, hoping I will someday become a man of tremendous faith.)

Unfortunately, it took several years and "significant pressure" for me to realize and admit I did have a "fleshly path" in my life that needed to be dealt with. I began to see that when emotional events or moments would occur, especially in our marriage, I would respond by shutting down. I felt nothing, and I could not relate to the intense struggle my wife was going through. That's a great quality for a pastor, right?

However, once I finally came to grips with my "ways" of coping with these moments and admitted I needed the Lord to help me, things began to fall into place. Karen and I had begun praying for the Lord to show me how to undo this "path" of mine. Not long after that, I was having breakfast with my parents. My mother began telling the story of my first four years of life. I won't go into the details, but there were about four or five extremely intense and even life-threatening incidents that occurred in our family: My father had cancer; my mother had a nervous breakdown; my brother was born prematurely, and both he and my mother were in critical condition; and there were several large moves (including to Japan and back) for the Air Force. I knew parts of these stories but had never heard them all put together. As my mother finished the story, she said something I will never forget: "In all this turmoil, you were the best baby!" she exclaimed.

Now, I am no child psychologist, but I know that was not right. Children are normally sensitive and alert to family traumas, and they usually act out the stress of such situations. She continued, "I could sit you in a corner, and you would just play by yourself for hours."

I began to realize that my "way" of shutting down in stressful and emotional situations had begun very early and became a well-worn "path" by adulthood. To me, it seemed natural and normal. My ability to withdraw was my "fleshly way" of coping, but not God's way. (Not incidentally, I was born without a tear duct in my right eye.)

If God had not brought Karen into my life to put "significant pressure" on this path, I am quite certain I would have sailed along on the surface not realizing my ways were not God's ways. I repented of coping with pain by withdrawing emotionally without turning to Him for comfort. He has begun to heal this area, and now I am able to feel! Hardly a worship service goes by that I don't deeply sense the heart of God for His people, and I often weep even in the middle of my sermon. I call it weeping; Karen says I just shed a couple of tears. She can *really* weep. And now I can empathize with her when she is hurting, and I am able to identify with others who are in pain and come to me for counsel. I still am very easy-going and a little "shallow," and I don't feel things to the depth Karen does, but that is who God made me. I am very grateful that healing has taken place in my life, so I can experience the joys and sorrows that are part of being human and being married.

If we misunderstand God's ways, we can wrongly react to the "significant pressure" He may be applying to our lives through our spouse and think or even say, "If only they would change!" God was at work in Karen as well, to be sure. He doesn't waste pressure. Through me, He was bringing healing to areas of her life, but it wasn't until we quit blaming each other for this pressure, and yielded to God, that things began to click.

I believe God handpicks a spouse for us who will bring "significant pressure" on just the areas He wants to work on. Often that means a person about as different from us as a turtle is from a hawk. If we are not careful, we will waste the opportunity to allow God to get us off our path—and onto His. The pressure is not fun; it is uncomfortable and frustrating, but it is necessary because we aren't easily dislodged from our paths.

Many people fight the pressure (and also the spouse) until the marriage ends sadly with the "fleshly paths" still very much intact. If they remarry, often that pressure is duplicated in the new partner with the same results. Others refuse to allow the Lord to shape them, yet they stay together, unchanged and miserable, just cohabitants in a house. Still others pretend to be happy, but inside them a volcano of resentment is growing. They can't be honest with their spouse, so they just swallow the resentment. These are marriages that end suddenly with the other partner totally unaware of the problems.

Psalm 139:5-6 says, *"You have hedged me behind and before, and laid Your hand upon me. Such knowledge is too wonderful for me; it is high, I cannot attain it."* Some of you feel ensnared in your marriage with no way out. You have committed your life to Christ and, for you, divorce is not an option. Still you feel trapped with a spouse who is continually putting "significant pressure" on you. You often are sure this marriage was a mistake, and you have to live with the consequences. I say it is God who has hedged you in and laid His hand upon you. You can give me a whole list of ungodly and fleshly problems with him or her and sound very spiritual as you make your defense. But God is more concerned with the right paths for you than He is with your living in marital bliss. When, and if, you will yield to the "significant pressure" God may be bringing through your "significant other," I believe you will find not only the "paths of God" but marital bliss as well.

Proverbs 14:12 says, *"There is a way that seems right to a man, but its end is the way of death."* Many of our own "ways" that we bring into marriage seem so right to us. We can eloquently explain why we're right and our spouse is wrong, when these ways are so different and opposite. We hold on for dear life to our position because if we feel that if we admit these ways are wrong, then everything about us is wrong. But, if they are just "our ways" and not "God's ways," then they will certainly end in death—in our marriage, our relationships, and existence in general. Help comes when we can admit, as the apostle Paul did in Romans 7:18: *"For I know that in me (that is, in my flesh) nothing good dwells…."*

When we can confess our desperate need for our Savior and really bring our fleshly ways to death, God can begin to remake us into that new creature He created us to be. We can experience the real life and future that He intends for us in marriage and all areas of life. With this comes the deep satisfying joy of living and walking on "God's paths." They really are, as Psalm 139:6 puts it, *"too wonderful for me"*!

God uses all sorts of things to bring this "significant pressure" on our ways to bring about the change in us that He desires. It just seems to me that marriage is one of the best. He connects a husband and wife through love and covenant in a way that holds us in place so the work can be done. We can quit jobs and move away from bothersome neighbors, but in marriage we are clamped in place so God can work.

I love to do woodwork and build things. When I need to sand the rough edges off a piece of oak, I usually clamp it in place so that the piece can be shaped as needed. I know it does not sound very romantic, but isn't that what God does in marriage? We are held in place while our beloved belt-sander of a wife or husband can be used to accomplish God's purpose.

The problem comes when we resist and react to the mighty hand of God and either run or fight. *Yield* is a powerful word. We see it posted on signs at intersections across the country. It means that we must stop and give way. It means that we must give way to another who has the right-of-way in our lives. In marriage we often refuse to yield because we see our spouse as the "other party" and a power struggle ensues over who indeed has the right-of-way!

It is not a sign of weakness to yield when we realize that really who we are yielding to is God. I am not saying that we are to become spineless and let people or even spouses walk all over us. The key is in slowing down and taking a moment to let God have His way.

I have watched couples, including Karen and myself, at an intersection of life battling for right-of-way, both refusing to give in or back down, neither wanting to yield to each other or God. When we have been able to stop, bring God into the picture, yielding to His ways, good things have happened. What if my spouse refuses to want to submit to God? Good question! Amazingly God works in us individually as well as corporately. I hear it all the time. If only my husband would be praying more, or if only my wife would submit to me, then our marriage would be great! In almost every case God is working on areas in both spouses. I almost always counsel them with what Karen and I have learned over the years of butting heads. You take care of your stuff and God will take care of your spouse.

"But you don't understand," they respond, "I am married to the devil himself." Okay, I am exaggerating a bit perhaps, but I have heard it in so many words. Most marriage counseling starts off with spouses tattling on each other. It is almost funny. There is a kind of "Wait until I tell the pastor what you are doing" attitude that comes out.

What I have found to be most effective is holding a kind of spiritual mirror in front of the face of each one. I try to reflect back to them those "fleshly ways" that God is after in them. Some refuse to see and walk away, angry not only at their spouse but now also at me. Many, however, are willing to look at those ways and repent. It seems to Karen and I that the more we each individually repent, amazingly the godlier our spouse becomes.

God will go to any lengths to get us to walk in His ways. He is much more concerned with getting us right with Him than He is with our comfort, our happiness, and our peace. If I can give you just one piece of advice that has come from over 33 years of walking with Him, it is this: *Give Up Quickly*!

CHAPTER 9

Hawk and Turtle Traps

The process of healing and restoration in our marriages takes time. It took years to get to the unhealthy places where we now find ourselves, and even if we think we will unravel them overnight, it usually doesn't happen that way. It has been my experience that the transformation process in marriage always takes longer than we think we can hang on. God will take as much time as is needed to do a thorough job of getting us right.

In this process, the enemy of our souls sets a snare that is designed to maim and even to terminate our marriages—envision a huge, steel bear trap with strong and jagged jaws. Once we find ourselves caught in it, escape seems nearly impossible. Jesus told us that satan, the thief of John 10:10, comes for a distinct purpose: to steal, kill, and destroy our lives and most certainly our marriages. This trap into which many of us have fallen is *bitterness and resentment!*

As a young boy, I did a little trapping. I caught some chipmunks and a few rabbits (and more skunks than I wanted). I am in no way an expert, but I did learn a few of the basic principles.

For a trap to be effective, it must be set in a way that the prey does not suspect that anything is amiss. It can't smell like a trap. In fact, we boiled ours to remove the human smell and carefully placed them wearing gloves so our prey would not be tipped off.

Likewise, if we could smell it, we would never knowingly put our foot into a trap of bitterness and resentment. But satan is no dummy. He has been catching humans in their natural weakness for centuries, and we are caught before we know it.

If you have been a Christian, for even a short time, you have probably had some teaching or training on one of the central themes Jesus taught about: forgiveness. It is our defense against resentment and bitterness. We are taught early on that forgiveness is not an option in God's Kingdom, and we must forgive those who offend us. Unfortunately, in today's world, I believe we have undervalued what true and deep forgiveness really means. The words, "I forgive you," are thrown around lightly and often not wholeheartedly. The Bible tells us we are to forgive others in the same way our heavenly Father has forgiven us. Well, how does He forgive us?

Here are a few ways:

As far as the east is from the west, so far has He removed our transgressions from us (Psalm 103:12).

For I will be merciful to their unrighteousness, and their sins and lawless deeds I will remember no more (Hebrews 8:12).

And of course, those incredible words that Jesus spoke as the men He came to die for drove spikes through His hands:

Father, forgive them; for they know not what they do (Luke 23:34 KJV).

Forgiveness means totally and completely letting go of every ounce of resentment and bitterness we hold against our offender. It is releasing them from our desire to see them punished or having to pay for their crime against us. It is clearing our heart of even the remembrance of the deed. Forgiveness is a choice, and it is hard!

Here is how I got caught. In God's using these distinct differences in Karen and me to transform us, offenses took place. Karen would blame me for our marriage being what it was. From time to time, she would come and ask me to forgive her. Ninety-eight percent of the time, being the good Christian husband I am, I would. The remaining two percent was unconsciously stored away in the deep recesses of my heart. If you asked me at the time if I was forgiving Karen, I would have said, "yes" and would have truly believed it. I did not realize that there was a growing reservoir of bitterness and resentment deep inside my heart; and with each little deposit, it was becoming more poisonous. I was being lured into a trap, and I didn't even smell it coming.

Meanwhile, Karen, being far more sensitive to these things, was feeling me pull away, and she sensed the wall growing between us. When she would talk to me about it, I of course denied it and told her it was her overactive emotions. I resented being accused, but I "knew" I needed to forgive, and I did—98 percent. The pressure continued to mount, in me and Karen. We were trying to work on our marriage and, all the while, this massive balloon of bitter resentment was swelling up between us.

One Saturday morning, we were lying in bed and Karen said something to me that to this day I don't remember, but I blew! With that last drop of unforgiveness and bitterness, the dam broke, and the floodwaters came gushing out. All those "two percents" had created a huge, vile lake. Years of stored-up anger and resentment came pouring out of my mouth. Jesus said it this way in Matthew 12:34: *"Brood of vipers! How can you, being evil, speak good things? For* **out of the abundance of the heart the mouth speaks."**

After I unloaded my fury, I stood shocked and in disbelief of the depth of bitterness and resentment I had stored up. Karen, also stunned, said these four little words that became unbelievably prophetic in our lives, "Now we can heal!"

It was a turning point in our marriage. I asked the Lord to truly cleanse my heart, all the way to the very deepest parts. I repented both to Karen and to God of the sin of holding onto this bitterness and resentment; and I made the decision never to let that happen again. Since then, I have tried diligently to guard my heart from this. Proverbs 4:23 says, *"Keep your heart with all diligence, for out of it spring the issues of life."* A number of times since that day, I have sensed some resentment in my heart towards Karen about something. I am quick to go to God and also to Karen and repent. It often means I need to talk honestly with her about the cause of the resentment. It is amazing how well God's ways work. If I have first taken the plank out of my own eye, as Jesus taught in the Sermon on the Mount, I can speak to Karen about the speck that may be in hers, without causing damage to our marriage.

It is impossible for two people to grow into the God-designed union of marriage, when any resentment or bitterness remains between them. It will poison and corrupt everything and is one of the chief weapons in satan's arsenal, since he is bent on destroying marriages. Many times, it grows undetected in our hearts (as it did with me) until true repentance can come. But don't let it build up and explode. It can cause serious damage to your spouse. I believe God's way is to come to Him not with 98 or even 99 percent. He desires us to walk in complete and true forgiveness. It may be one of the most difficult things in the Bible that we are commanded (yes, commanded!) to do.

The second principle of trapping that I learned is the importance of the right bait. If you want to catch rabbits, you don't use meat. If you want to catch a fox, you don't use lettuce. So what does satan use to catch unsuspecting men and women in the trap of resentment and bitterness? Self-righteousness, self-centeredness, selfishness...do I need to go on? It might come wrapped something like this: "You poor thing, you don't deserve to be treated so badly. After all the things you have done and put up with in this marriage. You have done more than your part. You have a right to be angry and resentful. It is time for you to stand up for yourself and take care of your needs!" Does any of that sound familiar to you? It is age-old bait that has been the undoing of many of us. We stick our heads in the snare and, before we know it, resentment and bitterness have caught us.

Offering true forgiveness is the most *self-less* thing we can do in our lives and marriages. It is following in the footsteps of Christ and patterning our lives after Him. It is the true mark of spiritual maturity and will bring tremendous growth in our marriages. Imagine a marriage with both people walking in true forgiveness. For many of us, we respond something like this, "OK! I am willing, but you go first." True forgiveness rushes to be first—it releases, repents, restores, and re-loves. I know that "re-loves" is not a word, but it should be!

I can almost hear you now, "But you don't know my husband," or "You have never met my wife, and you don't know how bad I have it." Yes, I do. I have met all of you. Names and details change, but the underlying story is pretty much the same. There really is nothing new under the sun, as Solomon said, and he had hundreds of wives. Our example of forgiveness and faithfulness is not in the marriages of this world, but in Jesus. Hebrews 12:3 says: *"For consider Him who endured such hostility from sinners against Himself, lest you become weary and discouraged in your souls."*

The entire chapter of Hebrews 12 is instruction and encouragement to us as to how to go through the discipline or training of the Lord. Hebrews 12:11 says: *"No chastening seems to be joyful for the present, but painful; nevertheless, afterward it yields the peaceable fruit of righteousness to those who have been trained by it."* (This chapter also tells us that, if we are God's sons, He will indeed chasten us. God's discipline is not punishment but rather training, and it is always motivated out of His love for us. So, yes, God gives us a husband or wife whom He will use to train us, even chasten us. They become His tool, since they are the closest ones to our hearts. He uses them to mold, sand, grind, and polish us.) The good news is found in several key words here in verse 11. *"Afterwards"* (when the discipline is complete) it will *"yield"* (produce) in us the *"peaceable fruit of righteousness"* (doing things the *right* way: God's way). This is a conditional promise, however, that hinges on the last phrase in the verse: *"To those who have been trained by it."*

In other words, you can go through the discipline of the Lord and not be trained by it. How many of us have disciplined our children for something, only to have them repeat the same behavior? They were not trained by the discipline.

Unfortunately, we often carry this same pattern into adulthood. With children, we continue to discipline and increase the consequences until they get it. Guess what God does with us?

A few verses later, we come to a very interesting warning relating to the way we endure God's discipline. Hebrews 12:15 says, *"looking carefully lest anyone fall short of the grace of God; lest any **root of bitterness** springing up **cause trouble**, and **by this many become defiled**."* Therefore, as God is training us through many different ways in our lives, including our spouse, we have to be very careful not to let a *"root of bitterness"* spring up in response to this training. I believe the picture here is best described as a poisonous weed. An awful weed called "napweed" covers almost the entire 30 acres our church sits on. The stuff is horrible! It is nearly impossible to kill, and it spreads like wildfire. Have you ever noticed that if you leave bare ground to itself, you never get neat rows of corn or tomatoes that just naturally spring up? We have a sin nature that will come to life and spread like weeds if we let our heart go its own way.

The next phrase, *"cause trouble,"* I think we can all relate to. Weeds are trouble! They are difficult to get rid of once they get established and, worse than that, they spread. Leave a single weed in your beautiful lawn, and it won't be long till you have a bumper crop. They produce seeds that can endure drought, frost, insects, and even fire. We had a wildfire on the church property a couple years back. As the fire department was hosing down the last few smoldering areas, we commented to one of the men that at least we burned the napweed. "Oh, no," he responded, "the heat just cracks open more seeds, and you will have a much bigger crop next year." Bitterness causes trouble wherever it is found, especially in marriage.

The last phrase may be the most important warning of all: *"by this many may become defiled."* The word *defiled* means "contaminated" or "stained." The bitterness we hold in our hearts toward someone not only causes trouble, but it can spread like weed seeds to other hearts. Left unchecked, our bitterness and resentment spills out and contaminates even innocent lives.

I am sure most of us have witnessed this, even in the church. Someone is offended and becomes resentful of another member or leader in the church. Instead of dealing with the matter as the Bible tells us to (and going to the one offended), the story of the offense is told to another. A seed of bitterness has just been planted in an unsuspecting heart, and soon a *"root of bitterness"* will spring up. If left unchecked, roots of bitterness soon spread throughout the body of believers. More than one church has experienced devastating splits because of this. Imagine how this affects our marriages. Roots of resentment and bitterness can spread to our spouse and even our children. They contaminate and stain our hearts toward one another, and does that cause trouble!

If, like the prodigal son, we find ourselves in the pigpen of resentment and the garden of our heart is overrun with bitter-roots, there is an answer to this terrible dilemma, praise God! It is the most wonderful word that provides hope for all of us sinners: **Repentance!** Join David in his cry to the Lord in Psalm 139:23-24: *"Search me, O God, and know my heart; try me, and know my anxieties; and see if there is any wicked way in me, and lead me in the way everlasting."*

The "way everlasting" is walking in repentance and forgiveness. The precious blood of Jesus is the best and only weed-killer for those wicked roots. Ask the Lord to search your heart for resentment and bitterness. Confess it to Him, and to others if need be, and receive His forgiveness as you forgive others.

CHAPTER 10

The Boundaries of Our Heart

T he Book of Proverbs is a collection of sayings of great wisdom—not just from human minds, but in reality the wisdom of God. Among the multitude of verses is one of my favorites: Proverbs 4:23 (KJV), *"Keep thy heart with all diligence; for out of it are the issues of life."* Some of the more recent translations say, *"Guard your heart, for it is the wellspring of life"* (NIV). During a study I was doing one day, I couldn't help noticing the difference in the translations, and my curiosity led me to a very interesting discovery.

The main difference seemed to be in the translation of the word "issue." Further research led me to the Hebrew word *towtsaah*, which is used 23 times in the Old Testament. From this word we get our English word "issue" and also "wellspring" or "stream." The word is used most often in the Book of Joshua, chapters 15–18, in reference to the land allotted to the 12 tribes of Israel. Oftentimes, a stream or river was the actual boundary— thus the translation of the word, in Proverbs 4, to "wellspring" or "stream."

However, the root meaning, it seems, is not the stream itself, but the border it becomes for the land of each tribe. The Lord had given exact boundaries to Moses who passed them on to Joshua (see Josh. 14:1-2). Within these boundaries, God had given each tribe an inheritance of land, which would define each of them as a people. Nothing more, and nothing less. It was their exact inheritance from the Lord. The big problem for Israel came when they did not take full possession of their allotment and left the enemy (or idol-worshiping people) on the land. These people eventually corrupted Israel and, in reality, stole what God had promised the Israelites. It was their gift from Him, but they did not receive it. Let's look at our Proverb, with this in mind.

This is what I believe the Lord had in mind in the writing of Proverbs 4:23: *"Keep and take full possession of all of your heart and inheritance from the Lord, for that makes up the boundaries of your life."* In other words, God has given each of us an allotment of life or a destiny for us to walk in. Within these boundaries, we are to *"live and move and have our being"* (Acts 17:28). There are, in a way, some restrictions God has placed on us, but also we have the freedom to take full possession of all that God wants us to be.

So, back to our "hawk and turtle." By His design and will, God has created within them a life and destiny with certain restrictions. Wouldn't it be wonderful if each of us took full possession of all that we were created to become? Unfortunately, most of us fall into the same trap as Israel did in not laying hold of everything God has for us as an inheritance. We let fear, unbelief, pride, and other idol-worshiping parts remain in us. Thus, many of us never reach the full potential of what we were created to be.

I believe that the enemies of our souls (satan and his helpers) are a big reason for this shortcoming. Jesus told us, in John 10, that the thief comes to kill, steal, and destroy our lives, our destiny, and our inheritance if he can and if we let him. Therefore the words of Proverbs 4:23 have come to have more meaning to me: *"Keep your heart with all diligence."* The word "keep," *natsar* in Hebrew, means to "watch or guard." We are to be diligent in watching over the boundaries of our lives, so we can be free to move and live anywhere within them.

As a citizen of the United States of America, I have the freedom to live anywhere I choose within its borders. I can move to Delaware or Arizona without permission or restriction. I am just as free to live within the borders God has created for *me.* He has given me a shepherd's heart, and I am free to live within the boundaries of *that* calling. He created me to be a leader, and I am free to move and operate within the parameters of that calling. But I must be faithful to guard and watch over my boundaries. I would not be honoring God if I were trying to live inside the borders of Karen's heart. She has a set of boundaries different from mine, yet just as important.

Boundaries define who we are, but they also define who we are *not.* As individuals, it is essential that we find out who we are in Christ and maintain, or diligently guard, those boundaries. The Bible is full of descriptions of who we are when we accept Christ as our Savior: We are forgiven; we are co-heirs with Christ; we are His beloved; we are protected, and so on. The problem arises when the enemy comes and suggests that we are *not* these things. He violates or perverts our boundaries. He tries to tell us we are not forgiven for the things of our past or that God really doesn't love us unconditionally. Or he may try to convince us that it's okay to allow a certain sin to remain in our lives and that it won't affect our relationship with Jesus. If satan succeeds in doing this, we cannot walk freely within the inheritance Christ intended for us because, just like Israel, there is an enemy (or a lie of the enemy) within our borders.

I have counseled many who have been lied to, and stolen from, by satan. In order to take full possession of their land, they had to drive out the enemy. This is done by repenting for allowing sin and unbelief to remain and by asking the Lord to forgive them for believing the lies of the kingdom of darkness instead of God's Word. Reminding them of who they are in Christ and exploring the person He has created them to be can also help bring freedom and fruitfulness in their lives. This then leads to a great joy of living and the fulfillment of being what Christ has created them to be.

Over the years, I have observed that there are certain patterns in the lives of people who have a hard time holding their God-created boundaries. One of these patterns is in those who have been abused, especially as children. The statistics that estimate the number of abused children are staggering: from 60-70 percent for girls and only slightly less for boys. This abuse can be emotional, physical, sexual, and even spiritual. When a child's boundaries are crossed, it sets the stage for an adult who has a difficult time holding those boundaries and who often even "expect" people to violate him or her.

A common example would be of a girl who was physically abused as a child. She grows up and may have a tendency to marry an abusive husband. It does not occur in every instance, but there is a definite pattern that can be traced. Many of us may wonder why a woman would leave one abusive relationship just to choose another man who is an abuser. Another instance would be a boy who bore the scars of a very controlling mother who grows up and then marries a wife with the same characteristics.

I believe it all comes from the essence of this Proverb. When our childhood boundaries are violated, then as adults we don't seem to be aware when someone else takes advantage of or abuses us in ways God never intended them to. When an animal (or some other force) breaks down a fence or wall, it gives access to off-limit areas. Boundaries set for a specific purpose are breached, and unwanted visitors can come in and cause great damage.

So, how do you undo this and reclaim the boundaries of your life God intended for you to guard and maintain? Isaiah 58 has some wonderful promises for those who are walking in obedience to God's ways. One of those promises is that we will become a *"Repairer of the Breach, the Restorer of Streets to Dwell In"* (Isa. 58:12). The first step is *recognition*, recognizing that your boundaries have been breached. I hope some of you may be having an "aha!" of why you have fallen prey to encroachment into areas of your life. I have heard some say, in effect, "Do I have a sign on my back that says *'Take advantage of me'*?" In a way, you do. The unspoken message you send is, "Here is a hole in my fence that someone else made, so come on in."

The first step is to repair the fence by asking God to help us forgive those who first breached the boundary and to repent for allowing it to continue to take place. Some of you may be saying, "Hey, buddy, hold your horses a minute! It's not my fault that someone abused me." That is true. We live in a fallen world and, in the lives of many of us, there are sinful, wounded, and even evil people. You may have suffered the most horrible and abusive situations that anyone can imagine. As a pastor and counselor, I have heard many heart-wrenching stories of abuse and neglect. Still, we are all responsible for *our own sinful reactions to whatever life has brought us.*

Certainly, many of us had no recourse when the abuse took place, but we are commanded (not requested) to forgive. Often, our first reaction is to hold unforgiveness as a way of punishing the one who violated us. We feel that it will somehow protect us from further abuse. This never works and just causes more pain and trouble. Unforgiveness keeps the fence broken down.

I have heard some say that holding unforgiveness is like drinking poison in order to kill someone else. It only hurts us and breaks our relationship with God. Jesus spoke so many times about forgiveness as being a key to maintaining an open flow of communication with God. In Matthew 6:9-13, we have the beautiful pattern of prayer that He taught His disciples. We have named it the Lord's Prayer, and most of us memorized it at an early age. Of the seven petitions included, Jesus ends the prayer with a special emphasis on the importance of forgiveness (and in the following two verses as well). As we begin to understand where our boundaries may have been breached, please remember that it is our responsibility to go to the Lord in repentance and forgiveness.

As I continue this chapter, I am all too aware that there may be some reading this who find themselves, at this very moment, in an abusive relationship. The circumstances and details are far too broad and complex for me to give a blanket statement as to the correct avenues to follow in reestablishing godly boundaries. I would encourage you to find a God-honoring, Christ-centered, and biblically based place to help you work through these very difficult issues.

Some of you may have a problem with thinking of "boundaries" as a good thing. I remember when I first heard this teaching, my reaction was, "Wait a minute! We are supposed to be Christians—bondservants with no rights. We are supposed to be laying down our lives for others, dying to ourselves, and going the way of the cross." Although these things are absolutely true and an essential part of our Christian lives, the understanding of "good boundaries" is also very scriptural. What may make our lives in Christ difficult to grasp is that there are often two opposite principles at work in us at the same time.

Let me give you an example. We are completely pure and spotless in the eyes of God, having received forgiveness of our sins through the atoning work of Christ on the cross. This is absolutely true and is forever. Yet, at the same time, we have a sin nature in us that is vile and desperately wicked, as Jeremiah states. Both these principles are true. The apostle Paul made statements like: *"in my flesh, dwelleth no good thing"* (Rom. 7:18 KJV), and *"Christ Jesus came into the world to save sinners—of whom I am the worst"* (1 Tim. 1:15 NIV). Paul took responsibility for the fact that he was a sinner and had a sin nature to contend with. He also made some very strong and powerful statements about who he was in Christ.

He opens many of his letters to the churches (the Epistles) with statements like this, *"Paul, an apostle—sent not from men nor by man, but by Jesus Christ and God the Father"* (Gal. 1:1 NIV). He made no apologies about who Christ had made him to be and the calling on his life. It was God's inheritance and gift to him and to the Church.

Even with Paul, there were those who tried to violate the boundaries God made in him. Some came against him and questioned if he had the right to be called an apostle. Paul walked in authority because he knew, not only in his head but also in his heart, who God had called him to be.

Much of the Book of Nehemiah is the story of the rebuilding of the walls of Jerusalem. It is an account of the restoration of the city. The walls of the city, or boundaries, had been broken down by the enemy, and God called Nehemiah to rebuild them. It is a spiritual picture of what God may be doing in many of our lives. Now I am not talking about the kind of walls we build out of self-protection, designed to isolate us from others. Those kinds of walls hinder us from becoming all God wants us to be. Rather, I am speaking of the walls, or boundaries, that define who, and for what purpose, God made us. To have healthy relationships and to walk in the destiny we have in Christ, we must allow God, not the world, to define the boundaries of our hearts. It is up to us to guard and watch over them.

It was shortly after my salvation experience that I began to sense that God had a call to church ministry on my life. I jumped at opportunities to be trained and develop the calling. I moved from Phoenix to Tucson to enroll in Bible college to continue my education—and to get as much experience as I could in ministry. About a year and a half into the program, I was asked to plant a church in southern Arizona. Karen and I had been married for only a month or so, but the leaders at the church and the overseers at the college agreed to send us forth.

Though I never "officially" graduated from seminary, over the next 25 years I continued to take courses and further my education through seminars and correspondence classes. I am quite sure that if I gathered together all the classes and credits I have taken, I would have enough to have a Master's degree in something. In fact, a number of times over those years I made an attempt at finishing the actual degree, yet each time, it seemed to me that God closed the doors on the process. I believe in education and strongly encourage it, but in my case God seemed to be saying that this calling and assignment of being a pastor must be settled in my heart. It was He who called me and He who defined me as a "pastor," not a degree or a standard set by men. I have gladly remained under the authority of the churches and leaders that God has placed over me, which is right and important before Him. (Unfortunately, there are those who, out of pride and rebellion, refuse to submit to the authority of the church and go off as self-proclaimed leaders. In most cases, there is usually little or no fruit.)

Over the years, there have been a few who have challenged my right to be an ordained pastor—some overtly, and some in a more quiet way. It used to really upset me and cause me to question my calling. Each time, when I would go to the Lord, He confirmed that He called me and established the borders of my life.

There was a time when I felt jealous of those whom I have now licensed or ordained into the ministry. We hold a special service and lay our hands on them to pray for them and publicly acknowledge their calling. We present them with an official document stating and recognizing the call. It is a good and holy thing. I merely received my license in the mail. I don't know why, but it seemed important to God that I should understand and walk in His authority without needing to have the seminary documents to back it up. I have also learned over the years that I do not have to defend myself. God has established me in my calling, and I have been blessed beyond measure as a pastor. I take no pride in this, as it is He who brought it to pass. My part has been simply to obey what He has asked of me. He has defined who I am and who I am not. If I allow others to tell me where my boundaries lie, it will be difficult to walk in the destiny God has for me. It is my responsibility to live within the scope of these boundaries. We can sometimes help each other discover God's destiny in our individual lives and assist and encourage one another to take full possession of that destiny, but it is God who has called us and known us from the beginning. He created us for His purpose.

I believe and have observed that when we know who we are and are living fully within the boundaries of our individual lives, it has a wonderful and positive effect on our marriages. We become the dynamic team that God created by calling us together: two individuals with unique callings, gifts, and borders, joined together to become a new and more extensive "land." It is two becoming one flesh, yet maintaining our gifts and callings as well as the roles God has asked us to walk in. Problems arise when, out of selfish or impure motives, we start to demand that our spouse be something God had not created. Often the underlying motive is to make us look better, or so we think.

Early on in our marriage, I realized that Karen is not your typical "pastor's wife" (whatever that is). I was tempted to want her to change to make me look more successful as a pastor. By God's grace, I quickly saw the error of my ways and resisted the temptation. Her uniqueness and specific giftings are what make us such a good team. I want with all my heart for Karen to become everything God has created her to be. To do this, it is absolutely essential that I maintain a clean heart towards her. David put it so beautifully in Psalm 51:10 (KJV), *"Create in me a clean heart, O God; and renew a right spirit within me."* When we have a clean heart and a right spirit toward our spouses without impure and selfish motives, we can encourage and bless them to take full possession of their inheritance. To me, a clean heart means watching my innermost thoughts and attitudes so I don't put my needs and wants over what God's desires are for *her*.

Just as important as encouraging and strengthening our spouses in everything God has called them to is helping them to see the things in them that are *not* there by God's design. I will come right out and say it: their sin. No one can see the blind spots of our lives better than our beloved partners. It is especially important that we maintain a "clean heart and right spirit" in this area: making sure our motives remain pure and our intentions right in helping our loved ones see that an enemy remains in their land. Our desire for freedom in our mates must first be based in a godly love for them, not simply an irritation for us. Again I think of the teaching of Jesus about "taking the beam out of our own eye before we can help remove the splinter from our brother's" works wonderfully in marriage.

I realize that this is so much easier to type out on the computer than to live out in real life; just ask Karen! There are things she has been patiently (and not so patiently) pointing out to me for years. God has used her and He has used me to bring repentance in many areas of each other's lives. Sometimes it comes with sparks—sometimes with tears. God has been faithful to help us drive out the sin and things in our lives that are stealing from His Kingdom purposes in us. It takes total commitment to the covenant promises we made to each other on our wedding day. It would be good, I think, to alter the marriage vows slightly: "...in sickness and in health, for richer, for poorer, for better, for worse, when you refuse to listen concerning your sin and when you do hear...I will love and cherish you!"

I would like to ask you to do a heart check-up on yourself. First, are you walking boldly in all the areas of life that God has designed you to walk in? Are you taking possession of your inheritance? If not, what are the "enemies" of God that remain? Have your borders been violated? Do they need to be reestablished? Consider asking a trusted friend or spiritual leader to help you through repentance, forgiveness, and the rebuilding of godly boundaries.

Second, are you doing all that God is asking of you to strengthen and encourage those things God wants your spouse to be? Do you have a clean heart towards them? Are your motives pure and right before God? Are you asking yourself those questions even as you read this? What do I do if my mate refuses to walk in all the things I can see that God has called him/her to? What if he/she refuses to hear when, with a clean heart, I come to try to help?

One simple (but difficult to carry out) solution is: Don't nag! Pray, and then pray some more. Do all you can do concerning your own destiny, and trust that God knows and sees your situation. Be faithful to your calling, while honoring your spouse and your relationship. Be sensitive to the Spirit of God about when to speak and when to remain silent in prayer. He is faithful, and though you may not understand the circumstances of your life, God does.

You may not see the plan and purpose in the spouse God has brought for you, but He does. You may be confused by the sometimes "strange ways" of the Lord, but He is not. Hebrews 10:23 (NIV) says, *"Let us hold unswervingly to the hope we profess, for He who promised is faithful."*

CHAPTER 11

Storm Watch!

If the truth be known (and we were being honest), most of us would confess to a storm now and then in our relationships. Whether it be in marriage or with close friends, work associates, or greater family members—where there are relationships, there are storms. For some, it would best be described as a gentle rain with some occasional gusts of wind. For others, it would be a category ten hurricane that rips through our lives on a fairly regular basis. Storms are a part of life, and those who say otherwise are living in a fantasy world.

Because storms are a reality, how we handle them is critical. If we do not prepare for them, storms can put intense pressure on a marriage relationship and can cause damage. Most of us do not come into marriage having been trained in "storm watch." The more different our giftings and personalities, the more intense the storms tend to be. Karen and I have had some major hurricanes in our day. Early on we thought for sure our world was coming to an end. As we have grown, we have learned how to go through them without so much destruction. Understanding that they are normal, and preparing for them, was essential.

I remember as a young boy living with my parents on Okinawa, a rather small island (67 miles long and between 2 and 7 miles wide), one of the southernmost islands of Japan. My father was in the U.S. Air Force, and our family was stationed there for a couple of years. There were loudspeakers on the air base that would warn us when a typhoon was approaching. They would announce that we were in condition one, two, or three. Condition three meant that we were to be in our homes with everything secured and that the storm could arrive at any time. My parents would prepare by putting plywood over the windows and storing clean water. As a youngster, for me it was mostly fun, but it was much more serious for them.

As an adult, I realize that preparation starts a long time before the alarm sounds—in many aspects of life. I have worked in construction for many years, and I am very aware of the work that goes into a foundation of a structure. Massive amounts of concrete are placed underground to ensure that the building can withstand the winds and rains of the storms that will come. It seems like a waste to put forth so much effort on a warm sunny day, when no sign of a storm exists. Yet we do it because experience tells us that the day is coming when an unexpected storm *will* hit. Jesus talked about it, and many of us learned this song in Sunday school:

The wise man built his house upon the rock…
And the rains came tumbling down!
The rains came down, and the floods came up…
And the house on the rock stood firm.

In premarital counseling, I try to prepare the couple for the inevitable storms they will face. If they have made a commitment to each other based on Christ as their foundation and have decided beforehand that with His help they will endure the storms, their chances for survival are good. The foundation of recognizing that their purpose in marriage is more about God's Kingdom than about their happiness will help them endure the storms that come. Also, learning to be flexible in their love for each other enables them to sway with the strong winds. And, above all else, the most important thing that prepares them to endure the powerful storms is their faith.

That's right! Without a doubt, faith is the one factor that will build an unshakable foundation for a marriage relationship. Our faith is not in the spouse we have chosen or in our own strength, but in Christ alone. Our faith is in the fact that He knows us and loves us and that our lives are in the palm of His hand. He is in control of our lives and is very aware of the circumstances we find ourselves in.

The storms of life have a way of testing or refining our faith in a way that nothing else can. That famous verse in James is one that we all love to quote but have a hard time living: *"Consider it pure joy, my brothers, whenever you face trials of many kinds, because you know that the testing of your faith develops perseverance. Perseverance must finish its work so that you may be mature and complete, not lacking anything"* (James 1:2-4 NIV). It is the testing of our faith that brings us to maturity, and God often uses our marriage relationships to develop this maturity. As Warren Wiersbe so accurately put it, "A faith that cannot be tested cannot be trusted."

Even in the natural, storms have some good effects as well. They tend to clean out polluted waterways and dirty skies. Storms can remove diseased trees and vegetation to make room for healthy ones to grow. Spiritually speaking, storms blow away the junk that accumulates in our lives: the resentments and unforgiveness we may be holding.

Storms get our attention. For example, the storm God sent as Jonah fled to Tarshish and away from God's calling had some positive repercussions. For him and his unsuspecting ship-mates, it really got their attention!

I remember one evening, while living in Northern Arizona, I headed off for an evening of frog-gigging. It was one of my favorite summertime events. I would take a flashlight, a long pole with a four-pronged gig on the end, and a gunnysack and make my way carefully around the swampy parts of the rivers. Bullfrogs are great eating, and sneaking up on the critters is a "blast." I went with a friend on this particular evening, and we could see a massive storm brewing way off in the distance. It appeared to be miles away, and I convinced my reluctant friend that we could certainly bag a few of the tasty amphibians before the rains came.

We were walking down the trail to the river with the ten-foot, metal gigging poles over our shoulders. Then, suddenly (and I do mean suddenly), a bolt of lightning struck the ground 100 feet from us with such force that it nearly knocked me off my feet. I turned to look for my friend, and I found him flat on the ground. The lightning had started a small fire, which we quickly put out with a shovel that someone had left nearby.

"Maybe it's not such a good idea to go frog-gigging tonight," I offered.

"You think?" he sharply replied.

Boy, did that storm get my attention! Often we cruise through life unaware of things that need to be looked at. God is after those things and is trying to speak to us about them, but often He can't be heard over the buzz of this frantic life. He *will* get our attention one way or another.

In Jonah's case, the storm caused the crew to throw cargo overboard. Sometimes, the storms of life can help dislodge things from our grip, things we were sure we couldn't live without. The crewmen, certain their lives were in danger, were more than willing to discard the "stuff" they were packing. Often in our prosperous lives, things take precedence over relationships. How many men sacrifice time with their families in order to earn the money to gather more "stuff"? But when faced with the loss of precious relationships, our toys seem to lose their glimmer. It helps bring life back into proper perspective.

Furthermore, the storm surfaced the sin that was resident in Jonah. As the storm intensified, the crew cast lots to see who the culprit was and to discover the cause of God's wrath upon them. The lot fell to Jonah. The crew gathered around him (I am quite sure with some stern and angry looks) and said, "What have you done?" Even the unbelieving sailors knew that a sin had been committed against God. When the sin was discarded (they finally tossed Jonah overboard), the storm subsided. There have been some mighty big storms that Karen and I have gone through that have had this same, very wonderful, effect. They have brought our junk to the surface and helped us to realize that we had sinned against God.

A recurring story has played itself out many times in our relationship. *Something was definitely wrong.* You could have felt the tension between us like static electricity. It is similar to those little glass globes that have the electrical charges going through them. When your hand gets close to the glass, it draws the juice to you and your hair stands on end. Things were ice-cold between us, to say the least, and neither of us knew why. We became short-tempered and were quick with sarcastic words and accusations. It would build for a while, and we made a couple of attempts at praying or talking it out. Then the storm would hit. As with Jonah, the storm seemed to bring to the surface the area of sin resident in both of us. We would discard the excess baggage we had been packing around. We would repent, forgive, and clear the air. There is nothing like the cool of the evening after a storm. The air is never fresher and cleaner, and so was our relationship.

Praise the Lord for storms! Somehow they seem to strengthen our resolve to keep on working it out. Like James put it, it builds perseverance, which is one thing every relationship needs. It leads us to maturity.

Jesus had some very interesting things go on during the storms He was involved in. In Mark, chapter 4, early on in His ministry with the disciples, we see amazing things: People are being healed, and He teaches with the authority of Heaven—revealing to the masses the very nature of the Kingdom of God. The crowd increases, and Jesus steps into a boat (to continue exhorting them) and tells some of His most famous parables. In verse 35, as evening comes, He says to the disciples (my paraphrase), "Hey guys, let's go to the other side of the lake." Then, Mark 4:37 (NIV) says, "A furious squall came up, and the waves broke over the boat, so that it was nearly swamped."

I have spent a great deal of time meditating on this story, and I am convinced that Jesus knew exactly what He was doing and was well aware of the coming storm. He is God, right? Then, of all things, we find Jesus sound asleep in the back of the boat. His disciples come to Him and wake Him with this very telling statement, *"Teacher, don't You care if we drown?"* (Mark 4:38 NIV). Jesus calms the storm with a word and says to His disciples, "Why are you so fearful? Have you no faith?" In this response, we see the clear connection between the natural fear that can come because of storms and the faith that Jesus was building and developing in His team.

Fear is the primary enemy to our faith. It can be the most destructive force in our relationship with God and each other. Let's look at three things the disciples did not understand about Jesus that caused them to fear.

First, the disciples were convinced that Jesus was not aware of the circumstances. In waking Him, they revealed that they didn't believe that Jesus was in control. Often in the storms of life we feel this way. Jesus seems to be asleep and completely unaware of our need and the urgency of the situation. In our marriages, it might feel like God has left the building and doesn't know of the torment we're in. Intellectually, we believe that God is all-knowing but, in our hearts, we hold fear.

Next, the disciples' cry to Him reveals the real fear of their hearts: *"Don't You **care** if we drown?"* How many times have we experienced this feeling within the scope of our earthly relationships? "God, if You really cared about me, You would intervene." The obvious conclusion? *There is either something wrong with me or something wrong with God.* Either way, it breaks our faith and erodes our confidence in our relationship with Him.

This may be one of the most difficult parts of God's nature for us to come to grips with. The Bible tells us that His ways are different from our ways and, compared to us, His thoughts are higher than the heavens are above the earth. When God is silent, our natural conclusion is that He simply doesn't care about us. To make matters worse, He has purposely put us smack-dab in the middle of a storm and gone to sleep. As a pastor, I am asked again and again about this aspect of God. The question may take on different forms, but the essence is the same: "If God is love, then why...?" (You fill in the blank). "Why does He allow a little child to die; why does He not stop the bloodshed; why doesn't He help me when I face the horrific storms of life?"

For the most part, I don't know why! I just know Him. I am growing to trust Him and have sometimes even joined Him at rest on the pillow at the back of the boat. Over time, my "freaking out" at the sight of storms has decreased dramatically. Remember, fear is always an enemy of faith.

Third, the disciples' first word revealed something hidden in their hearts. They yelled, *"Teacher!"* They had just witnessed Jesus tell some powerful parables and watched the crowd in awe over His wisdom. In that one simple word, I believe we see the essence of how they viewed Jesus at that time. If you recall, it was very early on in their time with Him. They were saying (again, my paraphrase), "Hey, You over there! You're a great teach' but don't know beans about sailing and lakes. You can really preach up a storm but can't do nothin' about one—and You sure didn't see this comin'! Hey, You who had the brilliant idea to head across the lake in the evening when storms often come rollin' through the area! Hey, wise guy, now what are we going to do?"

It is clear from their response, after Jesus spoke that powerful Spirit of God command, *"Peace, be still,"* they didn't comprehend Who they had in the boat: *"Who is this? Even the wind and the waves obey Him!"* (Mark 4:41 NIV). They did not yet understand that they were in the company of the Son of God, the Messiah, the Anointed One, the King of Kings, and the Lord of Lords. He's the One who spoke and created all that exists. It is amazing how small we can make God in our minds. Somehow, we assume that now and then He has a power shortage. We are sure that the struggles of our puny lives are more than He can handle.

In Paul's powerful prayer for the church at Ephesus, he asked for an expanded understanding of God's great love that is way past our knowledge, that they: *"may be able to comprehend with all the saints {that is, us} what is the width and length and depth and height—to know the love of Christ which passes knowledge; that you may be filled with all the fullness of God"* (Eph. 3:18-19). In other words, "God, please show us how big You are!"

Often when we find ourselves in the midst of the storms of life and relationships, our faith can give way to fear. With this fear come the same three questions of the disciples and an assault on the very nature and character of God. How is it, in the light of all God has done for us and the splendor of His nature, we have such little faith?

The storms can bring us to new places where God wants to take us and can demonstrate parts of His nature we would not otherwise understand. Another word the Bible uses for storms is the word "valley." They both can have the same kind of effect on us, if we will embrace them. Psalm 84:5-7 (NLT) says: *"Happy are those who are strong in the Lord, who set their minds on a pilgrimage to Jerusalem. When they walk through the Valley of Weeping, it will become a place of refreshing springs, where pools of blessing collect after the rains! They will continue to grow stronger, and each of them will appear before God in Jerusalem."* Sometimes God takes us into storms. Sometimes He takes into valleys. In these verses, we see Him taking us into a storm-in-a-valley! I have visited that valley.

There are some powerful spiritual principles about storms and valleys and God's use of them. In the valleys, there is weeping. Our soul cries out for God. Our emotions can become overwhelmed with our need for Him, and sometimes He seems silent. The pilgrimage to Jerusalem, which I believe represents our destiny in Christ, goes through the valley of weeping. In this Psalm, the word *baca* is used in many translations in place of the word "weeping." It is like a narrow, gloomy valley where brackish water trickles out of the rocks. Hence the "valley of weeping or oozing water" (*Zondervan Pictorial Encyclopedia of the Bible*). The valley is on the route that leads from northern Palestine to Jerusalem. It is a place none of us wants to go, yet we seem to find it on the road of our spiritual journey with Christ. The valley is dark and dangerous and closes in on us. It is a valley of struggle and difficulty, and we want out as soon as possible. God leads us there as He did Jesus at Gethsemane. It is unavoidable, but it is God's way.

If we remain strong in the Lord and set our hearts on following Him, He has some surprises in store for us in the valley. There are places hidden away in the valley that are refreshing streams—not brackish, undrinkable water, but fresh, cool, clear water that restores our souls. Just when you think you can't go on, your life or marriage is over, you are dehydrated beyond saving, God shows up! A refreshing spring! Springs don't normally pop out on the mountaintops. The water from the snow or rain works its way down to the floor of the valley where it finds a crevice to emerge from. It is in the valley that you find the spring.

The Psalm also states that in this valley *"pools of blessing collect after the rain."* "After" is the key word here. After the storm has passed, after the dark clouds have gone, only then will the pools of blessing collect. Water runs to the lowest point. It is often at our lowest place where we find the blessings of God collecting for us. Like springs, pools do not appear on the mountaintops. They gather in the depths of the valleys. Here God reveals His blessings and nature to us as nowhere else.

I spoke in an early chapter of the deep depression Karen experienced for many years. It was a valley of weeping, a storm she walked through with the Lord. He revealed Himself in a wonderful way, and He continues to use it in her life. Through her, God encourages others who are walking through this valley. She survived and knows the way. She found some refreshing springs and pools of blessing she can guide others to. I also experienced this valley, although in a different way from Karen. The Bible tells us that when we marry we become "one flesh." What one of us goes through deeply affects our spouse.

For me, watching my wife go through years of ever-deepening depression, and not being able to help, was one of the most difficult things I have ever had to deal with. I tried to help, but it became obvious that it was not I who held the answers. As Karen struggled more and more just to make it through the day, she was less and less able to meet my needs in our relationship. I felt as though I was in a no-win situation (and, in fact, I was). I had to fight not to become resentful with Karen for what she was unable to give me. At the same time, I felt guilty for even having needs, knowing how difficult it was for her. As I walked deeper and deeper into the valley of baca, my dreams of ministry and family life drifted farther and farther away. I was dying of thirst and saw nothing to revive my soul. As I have mentioned earlier Karen has often said to me that desperate can be our best friend. I began desperately searching for God, for living water.

It was a star-filled, warm evening when I found the bottom of my valley. I remember it as though it were last week, but it was over 14 years ago. I cried out to the Lord, and I gave up. I told Him I would accept His plan for me, no matter what that included. I gave up the right to ministry and family and my needs and collapsed onto the very floor of my valley. It was there I found the spring that has sustained me ever since. It was there the pool of blessing gathered for me to splash around in as much as I wanted to. As clearly as I have ever heard the Lord, He spoke to me through the words of two beautiful Scriptures:

> *Through the Lord's mercies we are not consumed, because His compassions fail not. They are new every morning; great is Your faithfulness.* **"The Lord is my portion," says my soul.** *Therefore I hope in Him!"* (Lamentations 3:22-24).

> *Whom have I in heaven but You? And there is none upon earth that I desire besides You. My flesh and my heart fail; but God is the strength of my heart and* **my portion forever** (Psalm 73:25-26).

It was if the Lord took my face in His powerful hands, like I was a two-year-old whose full attention He wanted. "I must be your portion and none other," the Lord simply spoke to me. "It is Me that you long for, and in Me you will find your hope. There is none on earth that you can desire more than Me. I am your portion! It is not Karen; it is not your children; it is not ministry; it is I. Therefore you have hope!"

I really don't know all that happened that night, but I found my spring! Since that day, I have not been the same. So many times over the years, I have needed God to be my portion, and He is and always will be. Things were placed in right order that night. I have needed this spring many times in the years that have followed, and I know where to find it. It never runs dry and is always refreshing to me. When the stresses of ministry and marriage have drained me completely and my flesh is failing me, God has been my portion. The wonderful part of this promise is in the last word of Psalm 73:26: "forever!"

Our natural inclination is to run from storms and avoid valleys at all cost. Don't! God is there.

And you will seek Me and find Me, when you search for Me with all your heart. I will be found by you, says the Lord... (Jeremiah 29:13-14).

CHAPTER 12

"Draw, Partner!"

We have all watched it many times on television and in movie theaters (for those of us who love westerns, we've seen it more times than other folks). The two cowboys meet at high noon on the dusty streets of an old town out west. Women and children run for cover, and men gather to see the outcome. The undertaker measures for a new coffin, and the moment of truth has arrived. A conflict has escalated out of control. It might be over grazing rights or a guy caught cheating in poker. Somebody has had enough, and all that is left is to see who will draw first and who is the fastest gun. No one is backing down and no one is surrendering. By sunset, someone will be six feet under!

By the time most of us are desperate enough to seek counsel in our marriage conflicts, we find ourselves face to face with our beloved partner—our coats pulled back and trigger-fingers twitching. The stories may change slightly, but the essence of the battle is the same. Both sides are sure they see clearly what the problem is and who needs to change. They may acknowledge that they might have a part in the problem, but they believe everything would be fine if only the other would surrender, repent, and start being the husband or wife God wants them to be. The lines have been drawn, and the stare-down has begun. Someone is going out feet first.

In reading this book, many of you may have highlighted sections you want your spouses to zero in on. You can hardly wait to get the book in their hands, so things can be put in order and you can begin living as God intended you to. If you are the hawk, you just can't wait to be released to fly and soar and finally be understood for who God has made you. If you are the turtle, you are relieved that hopefully a little grace will be extended and, just maybe, you won't be rushed through life. Each of you can see clearly now that (just as you suspected) your spouse is the problem, and you have been terribly misunderstood. Well, I have some good news and some bad news. The good news is that God is working deeply in the life of your spouse, and much of what you see may be accurate and may need to change. The bad news? It's YOU who are the real problem.

We may be ready to repent, but so often our repentance is conditional. We say, "I will take responsibility for *my part...*," all the while thinking that we are not the real problem. Adam had the nerve to say to God (when confronted with apple juice still running down his chin), "It was that *woman* **You** gave me." We can almost hear Adam thinking, "Hey, I am really the victim here! Yeah, I took a bite, but we wouldn't be anywhere near this tree if it wasn't for her! She's the one who fell for that line from the serpent; she's the one who picked the fruit and took the first bite. And by the way, God, it was You who gave me a faulty helpmate. I was asleep the whole time You were making her, remember? You designed her, God, so why should I get blamed? It's just not fair!"

We always want things to be fair. There is just something in us that demands it. We see it often in the lives of our children and (if we think hard enough) in our own childhood as well. Fairness was, and is, of the utmost importance in our lives. Dad brought home a candy bar for you and your brother to split. Painstaking effort was taken to make sure the bar was split exactly in the middle; yet, somehow, that was never quite accomplished. How many of you said, "That's okay, brother, you take the bigger half"? Not likely. We want to make sure things are fair! That goes for candy bars, birthday presents, and even the way God is now dealing with us as followers of Christ. Many of us may be willing to say, "I'll take responsibility for my stuff, but only if my spouse will, too." It is only fair!

Life and the Kingdom of God are not fair. Remember the story I spoke of earlier on in the book when Jesus confronted Peter with this very problem near the end of His time on earth. Let me expand on and recount it again as it is recorded for us in the last chapter of John. Here is the scene. Jesus had just appeared to the disciples who had gone back to fishing. The past month had been too much to handle. The arrest and crucifixion of Jesus had taken their toll, especially on Peter. He was probably trying to come to grips with the way he had let the Lord down at the most critical time. Then Resurrection Sunday had come, and everything had changed. He was risen and alive! And what did that mean to the faithful disciples? What did it mean to Peter? Would his relationship with the Lord ever be the same?

Suddenly, Jesus is there again. He had been showing up and then vanishing just as fast. Maybe I am reading too much into the text, but I can hear some frustration in Peter's voice when he proclaims in John 21:3, "Hey, I don't know about you guys, but I'm going fishing." I can picture him with his hand in the air and that edge in his voice that we all can relate to.

After a night of unsuccessful fishing, an unrecognizable figure appears to the disciples on the shore. It is Jesus, and He instructs them (as He had in the past) to try the other side of the boat. Once again, the nets are pulled in teeming with fish. Suddenly, John, who interestingly refers to himself as "the one Jesus loved" as he writes this, recognizes that it is the Lord. What a wonderfully confident relationship he had with Jesus! Peter swims ashore, and the famous breakfast on the beach takes place. Three times Jesus asks Peter if he loves Him, and three times Peter responds that he does indeed. At the end of each of his responses, Jesus tells him to feed the flock that would soon be under his care. Many believe this was the Lord's way of rein-stating Peter, after he had denied Jesus those three times.

It is in the next verses (18-21) that my point of fairness comes. Jesus immediately tells Peter that he will be required to give his life for the cause of Christ, and even alludes to the way he will die. He then offers to Peter the same invitation that He did at the very first: "Follow Me." Verse 20 records that Peter turns and sees the *"disciple whom Jesus loved."* Peter then, in verse 21, asks this very interesting and revealing question: *"But, Lord, what about this man?"*

I believe Peter was saying in essence, "It's just not fair! If I have to give my life for You, so be it, but how about him? You know, that 'Jesus-boy' who is always trying to snuggle up to you while the rest of us are doing the really tough work. He even calls himself the 'one Jesus loves.' I can't believe the nerve of that guy. Jesus loves all of us, but he thinks he's special. What about him? He is going to have to die too, right? After all, it's only fair." Jesus responds in John 21:22: *"If I will that he remain till I come,* **what is that to you?** *YOU follow me."*

What Jesus was expressing to Peter is a spiritual principle in the lives of all who have responded to His invitation to "follow Me." Certainly for all believers, taking up the cross and following Jesus is not an option. Neither is dying to our own fleshly desires. However, in God's Kingdom, the candy bar is rarely divided perfectly in half. God has different callings for each of us, and with those callings come different levels of sacrifice. It is not fair for me to sit comfortably in my office, sipping hot coffee as I type this out on my computer, while a Christian brother of mine in a dark corner of Africa struggles to feed his family. His church meets under a tree on Sunday, while we sit in 21-inch padded chairs. On a good week, the equivalent of one dollar comes in his offering.

It wasn't fair for Paul to be beaten and imprisoned for preaching the gospel, while others are given freedom. It wasn't fair for Job to go through the trials or for Joseph to be sold into slavery. Fairness is not really a part of God's Kingdom—obedience is! The Kingdom of God is not fair, but God is always just! Justice is a part of God's very nature. It comes from the Hebrew word that means "to be right." God is always right; His ways are right, and His plan for each of our lives is right. I don't understand why God might require my brother in Christ to give his life for the gospel, while I sit safely in my home. It may not be fair, but it is just and right because it is God's choice for each of us. Remember when we discussed what Jesus said, if we were to come after Him, we should deny ourselves and pick up our own cross and follow Him. I do not have the grace to carry your cross, nor do you have the calling or grace to carry mine.

Before I get myself in too much trouble, I should say that I am not calling your wife or husband a cross you must bear. In reality they may be, but only because they are instruments of God to help bring your fleshly ways to death. Everything in our lives that helps us in this process is a "beloved cross"—the greatest gift He could possibly give us. Never devalue the things God sends your way to help you die to your flesh.

If we take the principles of obedience and justice (not "fairness") and put them into the scenario of marriage or relationships, I believe great freedom can come to us all. Peter's attitude is often echoed in our showdown with our spouses. "Lord, what about this man (or woman)?" What God may be requiring of you will undoubtedly be different from what He is after in your spouse. As He said to Peter, "What is that to you? You follow Me." In other words, "You be obedient to what I have asked of you, and leave your spouse, or your boss, or your brother/sister in Christ to Me. You follow Me! Obey Me, and do what I have asked you to do."

It always seems to us that others are getting the bigger half of the candy bar. Sometimes they are. We are often just too self-absorbed to see it clearly. Most of us look at things through distorted lenses. We process everything through how it will affect us. That is not what Jesus taught His disciples. Laying down our lives, serving others, washing feet, and taking up our own cross is His way. Yes, this goes for marriage as well. In fact, it seems to work best in marriage.

I can hear many of you responding in your hearts with that famous "Yeah, but..." There is none of that in God's Kingdom. No "Yeah, but you don't know my spouse or my circumstance." ..."Yeah, but it's harder for me than you can imagine."... "Yeah, but I have already given so much, and my spouse is not even a believer." You can fill in the blank. We may have some great reason why this doesn't apply to us, but none of them works when confronted by the Word of God. It is not fair, but it is right before God to submit to His ways and plan for your life.

We may have married before we were believers, or in rebellion to parents or pastors who warned us against it. That doesn't give us license to abandon the marriage. God uses the circumstances of our lives to shape us into the vessels He desires us to be. Allow Him to take even the mistakes you have made and use them for His glory. God is *intimately acquainted with all of our ways*, David wrote in Psalm 139. He knows everything about your situation. If you let Him, He will use it to grow (and even bless) you and others.

Will every marriage be saved and every spouse respond with love and appreciation? Unfortunately, I think not. Because of our God-given free will and the sinful hearts of men and women, some marriages will continue to disintegrate and end sadly. There are no guarantees that even if we do all the right things, others will respond to God's moving. When we stand before God face-to-face on the day we leave this earth, each of us will have to give an account of the choices we made. We will not stand, according to Scripture, with our husband or wife there to point the finger at. We are each responsible for our actions and our responses to what life brought us.

"But, Lord," we might plead, "You had me marry a hawk! How could anyone have responded well to that? I would have to have been a saint." That's right—we are called to be saints, not because we have performed a certain number of miracles, but by living our lives in obedience to His Word. It's not "fair";

it is simply God's way. It's holy and just, and we can choose to be right before Him.

Walking in obedience is the call of all believers. The Word is very clear as to the standard and requirement of God's children to follow Him. We are to walk, not turning to the left or to the right. We are tempted to justify our behavior and/or lack of obedience because of our "situation." Those excuses don't work very well with Him. It is as simple as this: If we walk in a right way with God, the promise of blessing will come to us. Maybe not in the form we expect, but it will come. If we get off the path of God's ways and wander from His directives, trouble will surely follow.

The Lord gave me an up-close-and-personal illustration of this principle in just the past few months. After 10 years as the senior pastor at the church my wife and I planted, we were ready for a little break. Our founding board had had the wisdom to set up a sabbatical for us after 7 years. However, at that point, we didn't feel the church was in a place for us to leave for an extended period of time; but, after 10 years, both we and the church were ready.

We headed for the Oregon coast and worked our way down to a beach cabin just north of San Francisco to spend one of our weeks resting. One sunny afternoon, my son and I decided to play a little Frisbee behind the house. One of the tosses got away from me and landed in a patch of brush about 25 feet across. The Frisbee found its way into the very middle of it. It was no easy task crawling through the tangle of sticker bushes. Since it was the middle of January, I had no idea what kind of bushes they were, because none of them had leaves. The next day, I noticed a couple of spots on my legs that looked like insect bites. I assumed I had received them while crawling through the brush. I won't bore you with all the details but, within a week, both my legs were covered with blisters and rashes diagnosed as poison oak. Four weeks later, after several tubes of ointment, two prescriptions, and hundreds of hours of itching, the rashes finally began to disappear.

Karen and I had begun praying, shortly after the problem started, as to why the Lord allowed this. It just so happened that I was going through the Book of Deuteronomy in my daily Bible reading. Over and over, the Word would state: "Walk in My ways and be blessed. Disobey My ways and curses will come upon you." As I pondered these Scriptures and itched away, I could not help think about the "curse" of poison oak. When God cursed the earth after Adam and Eve sinned, I think He made poison oak and mosquitoes to be among the worst of the curses.

God gave me an illustration I will never forget. If you get off the paths He has set for you by disobeying His ways, curses will follow. When I got off the path and into the brush pile, I reaped the curse of poison oak. It's not like I was robbing someone's home or trespassing on another's property; I was playing Frisbee with my son. Why would God allow me to suffer so much for doing something good? It does not matter—the motive or purpose or the excuse. When we violate one of God's ways, curses follow.

I have listened to many couples explain why they decided to live together before marriage: to avoid becoming a divorce statistic. Sounds like a good idea, but it violates God's ways. Others have explained that they divorced because they wanted to serve God without the distraction of their "resistant" spouse.

No matter what our reason, God has established His ways for blessing and safety in our marriages. When we violate these ways, we will experience difficulties. It is His love for us to teach us to walk in His ways of blessing.

Early on, Karen and I were violating some of God's ways in our marriage. We were resisting the very thing He had given us—the precious gift of each other. We were not loving, honoring, and cherishing as we had vowed before God to do on our wedding day. We had gotten off the path and God, in His loving mercy, let us feel the full impact of our disobedience. That's right: *loving mercy.* Hebrews 12 tells us that those whom the Lord loves, He scourges and disciplines. Scourging? That can't be from God, can it? You bet it can! He loves us that much. He will allow us to experience the consequences of the faulty ways in our marriages, just as He did for me through my poison oak experience.

Interestingly enough, there was another lesson for me in this experience. After nearly four weeks had passed and the rashes were not really getting much better, my nerves were pretty much shot. Rashes are a horrible thing. I itched and scratched night and day, and I was really becoming worn out from interrupted sleep and the almost constant irritation. One afternoon, I decided to try my hand at getting on the Internet and checking out any possible help for my poison oak problem. This may be elementary to most of you, but for me to actually find something on the Internet is no small miracle. I somehow found a site featuring testimonials of people with bad cases of poison oak who had discovered some ways to help. One was using a common hair dryer. Those poor souls like myself had found some relief by blowing hot air on the rashes. They said to make it as hot as you could without burning your skin. As they had warned, it itched even worse for about 10 to 15 seconds and then, amazingly, stopped almost completely. It worked! I could go 10 hours itch-free. I would stand in the bathroom before bed and blow-dry the rash, which, by now, had spread over about 30 percent of my body. I could finally sleep a whole night through! Relief! Within a couple of days, the rash was disappearing, and healing was on its way.

You may be wondering what on earth this has to do with your relationships. Well, God seemed to be saying that it was the testimony of those who had suffered with the terrible plight of poison oak who helped me most. Desperation drove us to find a cure. When I was at the end of myself and willing to try anything to find relief, help was found. It was not primarily through professionals or medications, but through the testimonies of people just like me who had stumbled off the path into the cursed poison oak. Those who itched a long time and couldn't stand it any more gave me the help I needed.

This book is simply the story of our lives and the answers we have found that have brought not only great relief to us, but great joy as well. Karen and I are not experts in marriage relationships and communication. Nor are we brilliant theologians—just simple folks who have discovered some help for the struggles that God not only allows, but often ordains, in our marriages. We are simply in awe of His ways. We are amazed that He could take a couple of hard-headed, self-willed, rebellious knuckleheads and do anything good with us. God is amazing! We are just like those precious people on the Internet who took the time to write out their testimony and simply say, "Try this; it works!" I will be forever grateful to them.

I hope some of these things we have stumbled across in our marriage will help you find God's ways in your relationships. I hope that, like Karen and I, you will determine to hang in there in the dark times while answers are still unclear and just out of reach. Grab hold of Jesus, and let Him lead you through the difficult valleys of life.

So where do you start if you find yourself in a relationship like the one described in this book? A hawk and turtle in holy wedlock! Begin by thanking the Lord for His magnificent ways. Psalm 18:30 says, *"As for God, His way is perfect."* Thank Him for His holy plan for your life and for His choice of spouse or the person you are in relationship with. Hang in there, and don't give up. This may be one of the greatest opportunities you have in your entire life to face the "uglies" inside of you and submit to the work of the Holy Spirit. Embrace this precious gift from God to you.

Ask God to help you see things from His perspective, and rejoice in the balance that comes from two very different lives. Learn, as Paul said, to be content in the situation that God has fixed for you. Is that difficult? It may be the hardest thing you have ever had to do. But I promise you that you can't go wrong with trusting God and submitting to His ways. Let them shape you and conform you into His image. Stop fighting the current; turn around and enjoy the trip downstream!

Introduction to Study Guide

I have provided a list of study questions for each of the chapters in the book. My hope is that these may be used in a small group setting where couples, pre-marriage counselees, and others may openly discuss the topics in each chapter. I have used the word "spouse" to identify the relationship in question but this can apply to any close relationship you may currently be involved in.

These questions are designed to be thought-provoking and to generate discussion that may be valuable to the whole group. Please be open and honest. Transparency is contagious!

You may choose to use only certain questions each week for discussion depending on the size and makeup of your group. I hope that this will help you personalize the message and principle of the book.

Some of the questions may be a bit painful to look at. Ask the Lord to provide a "safe place" for your group to open their hearts up. Remind the group that confidentiality is an important commitment in order for people to feel free to share.

God bless,

Carl

1. What traits did you see in your spouse that first attracted you to them? Which of these traits appear to be opposite of yours?

2. Describe an "awakening" that happened in your relationship.

3. How are your opposite traits causing "sparks" in your relationship right now?

4. List some areas in which you and your spouse are becoming a better team.

NOTES

1. When has "desperation" ever motivated you to get help?

2. Describe an area where you have tried to coerce your spouse to be and think like you. What were the results?

3. Have you come to a place of acceptance with the distinct differences in you and your partner? Where are there still trouble spots?

4. Is there an animal that you would use to describe yourself? How about your spouse? Be nice! How would they get along in nature?

5. Have you come to a place of acceptance of who God has made YOU, and been able to celebrate that?

NOTES

DISCUSSION QUESTIONS
CHAPTER 2

1. How does the story of the hawk wanting the turtle to fly relate to your life with your spouse?

2. Are there traits in your spouse that you have deemed "wrong" just because they are very different from yours?

3. What are some ways you have expectations that they should change to be like you?

4. What are the traits in your spouse or loved one that you have grown to not only tolerate but truly value?

NOTES

1. In what ways do you and your spouse experience life differently?

2. How have you learned to rely on the particular gifts of the other to make a better team?

3. Do you tend to devalue the specific gifts God has given you and compare it to others?

4. How have you seen God supernaturally use you, overriding your natural weaknesses?

5. Do you lean more towards the area of self-pity or the area of pride?

NOTES

1. What "self" traits are still in you?

2. Give an example when being "self-right" caused you some trouble.

3. Have you ever thought of a meek person as having "strength under control"? Describe someone you know with this trait.

4. Is God able to guide you with His reins, or do you need a bit in your mouth?

NOTES

1. What has a higher priority in your life, to be happy or to be right with God? How can you tell?

2. Tell of a time when you chose God's ways over happiness in your relationship. What was the result?

3. When are you "blessed" (spoken well of) by God? Why or why not?

4. In what ways could God use you and your spouse's differences to enable you to be more effective for His Kingdom?

NOTES

1. Do you tend to look to your spouse in some areas of life to meet specific needs that only God Himself can meet?

2. Are there others in your life that you are looking to meet these needs? (friends, parents, children, bosses, pastors)

3. Is there a part of you that wants to be seen as a "savior" for others?

4. What do you need to do to get your marriage or relationships in right order in this area?

NOTES

DISCUSSION QUESTIONS
CHAPTER 7

1. Can you identify in your life, a well-worn path that needs to be transformed?

2. After reading this chapter, do you see any of "your ways" that God is wanting you to let go of?

3. Do you believe that God can take you and your spouse, who may have dramatic differences, and cause you to dwell together in peace and safety?

4. What would you need to know about God in order to "let go" of the branch you may be hanging onto?

NOTES

1. What are some of the fleshly ways or patterns (dealing with life's problems apart from God) you see in your own life?

2. What are the first steps in allowing God to help you change these ways?

3. How is God using your spouse to put "significant pressure" on you to change these ways? How are you responding?

4. Are there areas in your marriage that you have been able to yield to this pressure from God and see change?

NOTES

1. How can you tell when bitterness or resentment is in your heart towards your loved one?

2. What usually happens in your relationship when these are left unchecked?

3. What do you do if your spouse or loved one continues to offend you in the same areas? What is the biblical or godly response to this?

4. How do the principles of forgiveness found in the Bible apply to the marriage relationship?

NOTES

DISCUSSION QUESTIONS
CHAPTER 10

1. Are there some God-created boundaries in your life that have been violated? Have there been any patterns of this?

2. What does your promised land (destiny for your life) look like?

3. How does the landscape of your spouse's life complement yours? (An example would be my broad view of things and Karen's more specific view.)

4. Are there any areas of God's promises in your life that you have not been able to take possession of? Why?

NOTES

1. What is your natural response to the storms of life?

2. How do you and your spouse respond differently to storms?

3. Have you ever found a spring in the "valley of weeping" that God has used to give you strength and teach you His ways?

4. If "faith" is our best preparation for storms, how can you build faith in your relationship and in life?

5. What do you see God doing in the storms and valleys of your life and how can you cooperate with Him?

NOTES

1. Have you and your spouse ever found yourselves in a "showdown" like the one described in this chapter?

2. What do you see as the differences between being fair and just?

3. Do most of your conflicts in your relationship usually revolve around the same general area? What does that tell you?

4. What are some of God's ways that you may be violating that are causing some conflicts in your relationship?

5. Can you see with eyes of faith that God has a wonderful plan in store for you and your spouse?

NOTES

Author Contact Page

Pastor Carl Hampsch
P.O. Box 665
Newman Lake, WA 99025
wordlifechurch@juno.com

Additional copies of this book and other
book titles from DESTINY IMAGE are
available at your local bookstore.

Call toll-free: 1-800-722-6774.

Send a request for a catalog to:

Destiny Image® Publishers, Inc.
P.O. Box 310
Shippensburg, PA 17257-0310

*"Speaking to the Purposes of God for this
Generation and for the Generations to Come"*

For a complete list of our titles,
visit us at www.destinyimage.com